We're Having a
REORG
NOW WHAT?

Nicole Labbe and Christine Strobele

 FriesenPress

Suite 300 - 990 Fort St
Victoria, BC, V8V 3K2
Canada

www.friesenpress.com

Copyright © 2020 by Nicole Labbe and Christine Strobele
First Edition — 2020

All rights reserved.

No part of this publication may be reproduced in any form, or by any means, electronic or mechanical, including photocopying, recording, or any information browsing, storage, or retrieval system, without permission in writing from FriesenPress.

ISBN
978-1-5255-6862-6 (Hardcover)
978-1-5255-6863-3 (Paperback)
978-1-5255-6864-0 (eBook)

1. BUSINESS & ECONOMICS

Distributed to the trade by The Ingram Book Company

MANAGING THROUGH TURBULENT TIMES AT WORK

TABLE OF CONTENTS

Introduction – The Hidden Face of Reorganizations..... 1

Chapter 1 – Announcing a Reorganization.................... 7

    Is there a good way to announce a reorganization involving job losses? 12

    The most common approaches for announcing a reorganization 16

    Limiting the damage caused by the announcement 24

    The announcement day 27

    When reality hits 32

Chapter 2 – Survivors of a Reorganization.................. 39

    What is survivor syndrome? 42

    Recognizing survivor syndrome 45

    Manifestations of survivor syndrome 47

    Employee loyalty following a reorganization 52

    Impact of a demotion 53

    Managing stress 55

    Becoming resilient 58

    When resilience unravels 60

    Workplace disengagement 61

    Dealing with disengagement 64

Chapter 3 – Ensuring the Success of the Team Following a Reorganization............ 71

Impact of company's control mechanisms.................... 73
What is the profile sought for a team leader following a reorganization? 78
Emotional intelligence................................. 80
Becoming an effective collaborator 86
Day 1 following a reorganization 93
Succeeding as a team leader.. 99

Chapter 4 – Working on My Development.................. 103

Discussing the psychological contract with my boss....... 104
Taking control of my career development.................. 106
Overcoming a toxic work atmosphere 110
Ideas for surviving post-reorganization: the survivor's toolboxes... 112

Conclusion – Surviving change by thriving through change 121

Introduction

THE HIDDEN FACE OF REORGANIZATIONS

Companies must continuously adapt to new technologies and market dynamics. In some situations, like the global economic crisis created by the COVID-19 pandemic, companies are forced to adjust and adapt with little notice. Downsizing (or "rightsizing," as it is called by corporate pundits) is often considered "healthy management," necessary to reduce expenses and maintain a healthy bottom line. Consequently, workplace reorganizations are now part of the daily lives of many employees.

Several terms are used by the senior leadership to communicate information related to organizational changes within a corporation. They talk about transformation, re-engineering, reorganization, transferring activities, department mergers, financial austerity measures, globalization of operations, shake-ups, resource optimization, etc. Any one of these is likely to happen during the course of a company's life cycle because the work environment must constantly adapt to remain competitive. Implementations of new technologies, like artificial intelligence, will only ensure these transformations continue. Do those organizational changes always deliver their initial promises successfully? Unfortunately, research shows that 80% of companies fail to achieve their desired results in the time planned.

Why do reorganizations occur so frequently, especially when such disruptions often fail to deliver? Certainly, poor planning and execution of the reorganization are key contributors, but the most important, and usually neglected, culprit is the underestimated impact of the changes on employees and managers.

Let's look at it from the employees' perspective. Initially, they experience intense stress over the possibility of losing their jobs, which has a direct impact on their attitudes and behaviors at work. During the course of the reorganization process, some will have to leave, while others will remain with the company. Understanding the complex adaptations that lie ahead, one might wonder which group are really the lucky ones. Those who stay will have to watch their colleagues leave; they will have to grow into the new organizational structure, which will frequently involve changes in their roles, expertise, and responsibilities. Research suggests that the ensuing uncertain work environment provoked by organizational changes causes greater stress and anxiety than the actual layoffs that occurred. First-line managers and their employees, for example, are often the ones who keep the ship afloat during these periods of uncertainty. It falls upon them to get all of the basic work done with less infrastructure, to maintain the company's productivity while preserving the relationships with clients.

Human beings have always demonstrated an extraordinary ability to adapt, but deep down, people are looking for stability. Each employee is affected by layoffs within their department to varying degrees. Finding themselves with another manager or a new work team is stimulating for some, yet unsettling for others. The need to develop relationships, adjust to the many corporate and departmental changes, to learn new tasks quickly, redefine priorities, handle an increased workload, and take part in training sessions—all happening at the same time—is very stressful. The organization expects the employees to become proficient and productive as soon as possible. Moreover, there is always a certain amount of ambiguity to overcome with respect to the assignment of roles and responsibilities following the implementation of a new organizational structure. In short, the new work environment requires adjustments and creates uncertainties that result in additional effort demanded of each employee.

What will happen in the days immediately following the announcement of a reorganization, when the still-employed return to work? They will suppress their emotions and continue as if nothing has happened. They will project a positive and enthusiastic attitude in order to hide their anxiety, while experiencing sleeping difficulties and mood swings. In their new environment, they will become increasingly nervous about making mistakes. Walking on eggshells, they will become less motivated about cooperating with others. These behaviors are the hallmark of survivor syndrome. As workplace reorganizations are now part of the daily lives of many employees, these survivors are facing important challenges that if unrecognized and unaddressed, result in the development of survivor syndrome.

Let's be clear from the start: survivor syndrome is not an employee whim or a sign of weakness. Any employee who survives a reorganization involving job cuts or important changes in their department will have to deal with one or more behaviors related to survivor syndrome. It's inevitable, and has to be recognized. Symptoms can appear in the days following the announcements, or weeks later. They can affect the person in their personal life or even in the manner in which they behave at work. Survivor syndrome can lead to burnout. Interestingly, its first manifestation is generally denial, a refusal to recognize any symptoms at all, because most people are not even aware of survivor syndrome. People view themselves as "strong, solid, unshakable" in order to remain motivated, or look good for their bosses. In many cases, it is family and friends who notice that the "survivor" has sleeping difficulties, is less enthusiastic, and has less energy than before. At work, the atmosphere is heavier, people laugh less, some have a tendency to isolate themselves, and they steer clear of making difficult decisions so as to avoid making errors. It contributes to the development of a work environment that is stressful, demotivating, and can lead directly to an attitude of disengagement. As it turns out, the winners of the reorganization lottery are not necessarily those who keep their jobs!

The challenge when dealing with survivor syndrome is that most organizations are not aware of it—mainly because they have not been trained to recognize or address it. Survivor syndrome is an important contributing factor that explains why corporations fail to deliver on their promises following a reorganization.

How can the impact of survivor syndrome be minimized? Several easy-to-apply solutions are explained throughout this book that will help both the employees and the managers navigate this turbulent period.

One of our goals is to explain the concept of survivor syndrome on a personal and professional level, so that it can be readily recognized and addressed. We will discuss the role of the manager, who is also a survivor and has to supervise a team of survivors. We will explain the consequences of the organizational changes in the lives of the front-line employees and managers, while sharing our thoughts and observations, born of our experience as both employees and team leaders who have lived through several such upheavals. Our book offers tips and ideas to overcome the challenges of working in this continually changing environment.

We focus primarily on reorganizations in the private sector, with a few references to situations in the public sector. Our approach is to open several windows that will enable readers to recognize their situations, make connections, and identify strategies that will satisfy their particular needs.

This book is written in the format of a practical guide. It comprises four chapters. The first covers different ways to announce a reorganization, and their various impacts on employees. The second chapter provides information about the aspects of survivor syndrome and discusses ways for managing stress better, and developing an attitude of resilience. It also covers the subject of the loss of engagement at work. In the third chapter, we propose a set of additional skills required by a team leader to perform better in an environment of workplace flux. It introduces concepts of emotional intelligence and efficient collaboration that benefit all team members. Chapter three also discusses how to approach Day One following a reorganization, and how to build a performing team. The last chapter, chapter four, suggests practical solutions and strategies for self-development in the challenging post-reorganization environment. It provides tips for discussing the employee-employer psychological contract, and taking control of individual career development. It also addresses challenges of working in an atmosphere that has almost inevitably become toxic. Finally, the survivor's toolbox shares ideas for the regaining of personal satisfaction at work.

This book is intended for all types of employees, including managers who want to prepare to overcome the challenges of a reorganization at work, and all other employees who want to learn about how survivor syndrome could affect them. The approach is practical, and concrete examples are provided. The writing of this book was motivated by our professional expertise born out of personal experience, our curiosity to learn and conduct in-depth inquiry and, above all, to fulfill the need expressed by employees and managers for help through these stressful and disruptive times at work.

To illustrate the extent of our expertise, both coauthors, Nicole Labbe and Christine Strobele, have survived many reorganizations during their careers. Nicole has survived seven over a period of fifteen years, and Christine has survived five over ten years. Our similar experiences reinforce our perspectives, enhanced by testimonials from individuals who have faced similar challenges.[1]

Putting the strategies that we have set forth in this book into action will enable both employees and managers to successfully navigate turbulent times, and create productive and rewarding work environments for everyone once again.

We hope our book will help you manage through the turbulent times at work caused by a reorganization.

---

[1]. All testimonials have been modified to protect the identity of the individual.

Chapter 1

ANNOUNCING A REORGANIZATION

When explaining survivor syndrome in a work environment, author and researcher David M. Noer provided a useful family analogy that conveys a better understanding of the emotions experienced by employees and managers going through a reorganization with job losses. It highlights what happens when organizational changes are announced:

> Imagine a family: a father, a mother, and four children. The family has been together for a long time, living in a loving, nurturing, trusting environment. The parents take care of the children, who reciprocate by being good. Every morning the family sits down to breakfast together, a ritual that functions as a bonding experience, somewhat akin to an organizational staff meeting. One morning, the children sense that something is wrong. The parents

exchange furtive glances, appear nervous, and after a painful silence, the mother speaks. "Father and I have reviewed the family budget," she says, looking down at her plate, avoiding eye contact, "and we just don't have enough money to make ends meet!" She forces herself to look around the table and continues, "As much as we would like to, we just can't afford to feed and clothe all four of you." After another silence, she points a finger: "You two must go!"

"It's nothing personal," explains the father as he passes out a sheet of paper to each of the children. "As you can see by the numbers in front of you, it's simply an economic decision. We really have no choice." He continues, forcing a smile, "We have arranged for your aunt and uncle to help you get settled, to aid in your transition."

The next morning, the two remaining children are greeted by a table on which only four places have been set. Two chairs have been removed. All physical evidence of the other two children has vanished. The emotional evidence is suppressed and ignored. No one talks about the two who are no longer there. The parents emphasize to the two remaining children, the survivors, that they should be grateful, "since, after all, you've been allowed to remain in the family." To show their gratitude, the remaining children will be expected to work harder on the family chores. The father explains that "the workload remains the same even though there are two fewer of you." The mother reassures them that "this will make us a closer family!" "Eat your breakfast, children," entreats the father. "After all, food costs money!"[2]

How do the remaining children feel? This family story is very similar to what employees experience during a reorganization involving job cuts. It is difficult to see colleagues with whom one has developed bonds leave the company, and it is stressful to take on the workload of colleagues who have left.

Whereas twenty years ago a layoff announcement was viewed as a catastrophe, today companies refer to it as healthy management. What a change in perception! For employees, this represents a dreaded period of stressful uncertainty. To illustrate the influence of this new reality, an analysis conducted by McKinsey showed that "approximately 60% of companies in the S&P 500 have launched large-scale cost-reduction and reorganization initiatives within the past five years."[3]

A question that comes to mind is why do reorganizations occur so frequently? The reasons for the decision to reorganize may be strategic, economic, or technological: today's businesses are under constant pressure to perform to meet shareholder expectations through the merger of two companies or departments, a change in strategic direction, a new management team, discontinued products or promotion of a new product, changes

---

2. David M. Noer, *Healing the Wounds,* (San Francisco: Jossey-Bass, 1993), 8.
3. Camilo Becdach, Shannon Hennesy, and Lauren Ratner, "Rethinking the rules of reorganization," *McKinsey & Company* (April 2016), www.mckinsey.com.

in the competitive landscape, implementation of new technologies, globalization of processes, subcontracting, optimization of resources, cost reduction, etc. Executive leadership and the board of directors are the ones who make the decision to restructure the organization. This is a conscious and intentional choice, one made to improve organizational efficiency, reduce expenses, and increase shareholder profits. In order to attain these objectives, in financial terms, reducing the number of employees is an effective short-term solution. All types of businesses or public services, regardless of their size, could face such a reorganization that requires job cuts. Regardless of the reason, though, the fundamental motives for those making such a decision are profitability and increasing the company's market value.

Researchers Stephane J. G. Girod and Samina Karim published an article in the *Harvard Business Review*, entitled "Restructure or Reconfigure," on the financial impact of a reorganization within a large corporation.[4] Their research demonstrated that a reorganization results in an average loss in profits of 2.6%. The companies that come out of a reorganization most successfully needed three to four years to reap the benefits of their decisions. Other research showed that only a few reorganizations have been successful: "according to a McKinsey survey, more than 80% fail to deliver the hoped-for value in the time planned, and 10% cause real damage to the company."[5] These figures are impressive, and should provide food for thought! In order to achieve financial success after organizational changes, consideration and attention must be given to the significant impact it has made on the employees' attitude and engagement level at work.

---

4. Stephane J. G. Girod and Samina Karim, "Restructure or Reconfigure?" *Harvard Business Review*, Vol. 95, No. 2 (March–April 2017): 128–132.
5. Steven Heidari-Robinson and Suzanne Heywood, "Getting Reorgs Right," *Harvard Business Review*, Vol. 94, (November 2016): 84–89.

In most reorganizations, there are employees who lose their jobs and others who keep theirs. We would like to introduce a third category of affected employees: those who still have a job, but are no longer working for the same organization. They are now employees of a third party contracted by their former employer. This happens when a company decides to subcontract the services previously conducted by a specific internal department.

> Darren, an IT specialist, says this: *"I held the same position within an organization for ten years, but my employer changed last year. The company decided to subcontract the IT support services provided by my department. I still have a job for the same salary. However, my benefits melted like snow in the spring. So did my pension plan. My motivation at work has flown out the window."*

The company reorganized and saved costs by moving an in-house function to an external subcontractor. Darren kept the same job and works with the same colleagues, but he has a new employer, so he is still considered a survivor; the reorganization impacted him in other profound ways, resulting in a change in his behavior and attitude at work. Beyond the strategic decisions made by management, any organizational changes have significant impact for those who remain with the company. The employees' commitment to their work and their employer will never be the same. We will discuss the topic of employee engagement further in Chapter 2.

Is there a good way to announce a reorganization involving job losses?

There is no magic formula to announce an organizational change, but there are good practices that will limit the damage and ensure optimal and transparent communication that respects all of the employees. Any announcement or rumor involving job losses significantly increases the employees' level of anxiety and uncertainty. For an employee, this is the most difficult type of stress to manage, regardless of their position in the hierarchy. It takes only a few minutes for the work environment to change drastically; a climate of distrust settles in as each employee hopes to be among the survivors—who will be saved from the layoffs.

When the termination of an employment relationship is announced, the situation is difficult for everyone involved. It is not just the employees losing their jobs who are affected; all employees will experience the collateral impact of the reorganization. It is in the best interest of the managers to prepare thoroughly for communicating the reasoning behind the reorganization in a transparent manner to all employees. The manner in which the employees who are to lose their jobs are treated will have a direct impact on those who will remain with the company. These survivors will also need support and explanations about the reason for the reorganization and the company's resulting new vision. All too often, the survivors are told to come back to work the day following a reorganization with a "business as usual" attitude, as if nothing had happened. This is a strategic error on the part of management, and it will have negative consequences on the work atmosphere, the employees' level of commitment, and subsequently, the company's ability to attain its objectives.

Testimonials given, along with our experience, have helped to develop the next installment in the family analogy described at the beginning of this chapter, illustrating the impact of the announcement of a reorganization involving job cuts following a corporate merger:

> Two years later, our initial family breaks up and the parents rebuild their lives, each with a new partner. So, we find a reconstituted family with the father, his new wife, and eight shared children. The two children who survived the first round of abandonment managed to rebuild some of their trust in their father, but they remain fragile. The family atmosphere seems serene and collaborative: the older children act as mentors to the younger ones. There is even a rotation of duties so as to enable each child to expand their knowledge and build on their skills.
>
> In recent months, economic growth has slowed and the family's income has melted. As good managers, the parents have reduced their expenses by scrutinizing each expense in detail. Despite everything, this strategy has not been enough, and the family's indebtedness has reached a peak. One day, they write an email to their children, stating that the family's financial situation is not sustainable. Two children will have to leave the home within six months if the situation does not improve. Only the best performing children will be able to remain at home.
>
> Immediately, the children feel stressed and anxious. No one wants to leave home. This announcement

has pulled the rug out from under them. What should they do? The parents reassure them, telling them to keep on doing what they were doing as if nothing has changed. However, the children feel like there is a dark cloud hanging over their heads and that any error or slackening of effort on their part will be punished.

In the following weeks, the children's behaviors and attitudes change as a result of the additional stress. One of the children grows increasingly isolated from the family and spends most of the day in his room. He does the absolute minimum he is required to do;[6] his sister is just the opposite. Anxious and a perfectionist by nature, she works nonstop and even works overtime to perform the tasks left undone by the others. Her sleep is disrupted and she is exhausted. The mutual assistance that was once part of the family's values is no more. The children trust one another less and less. They even go so far as to denounce those who don't do their work correctly. The younger children find themselves having to do tasks that they have never done before that they don't have the experience to do. They can no longer rely on their older brothers and sisters for help.

Seeing the children express their frustration more and more frequently, the parents decide not to tolerate any negative comments or attitudes. "After

---

6. The usage of "he" refers to both genders throughout the book.

all, we're a family and we have to look happy so as not to alert our neighbors," says the father. The children get the message. They develop shells so as to protect themselves against anything that is negative. They start to see their situation through rose-colored glasses. When the parents ask them how it's going, they reply that everything is fine, everything is perfect, and they're happy!

In the days preceding the target date for the announcement, the children attain a level of stress that is difficult to manage. They work as little as possible. Each child sits locked up in their room, staring at their cell phone and their computer, looking for the slightest indication as to what their parents' decision will be. The rumor mill is operating full time, relaying all kinds of catastrophic scenarios.

D-day arrives. The parents have asked the children to stay in their rooms. Only the children who have to leave the home are met with individually. As soon as a child is summoned to the parents' office, the footsteps in the corridor arouse suspicions, and the other children find out who is concerned by peeking through half-open doors. At 6:00 p.m., the parents invite the surviving children to a large family dinner. The parents are joyful and dynamic; they present a superb video to the surviving children explaining that the family's short-term future has been saved as a result of their new strategy and that they should be glad to remain in the family since they are the best! No one talks about the children who left.

Will the children emerge from this new trial unharmed? How committed will they be to their amputated family? What will the environment at home be like in the coming months? Will the family survive the breach in trust between the parents and the children?

Yes, this analogy is a shocking one, but, since many employees consider their workplace a "second" family, it is a good example for illustrating their distress in the face of an organization change. This analogy is intended to highlight the key elements of a reorganization, namely:

- ✓ stress and anxiety are experienced by all the individuals involved
- ✓ isolation and limited cooperation from employees
- ✓ economic factors justifying the decision
- ✓ a breach in trust between managers and employees
- ✓ employees not acknowledged and left alone
- ✓ additional workload and a lack of expertise for performing certain tasks
- ✓ repressed emotions in order to keep up appearances
- ✓ a loss of control over one's work

The most common approaches for announcing a reorganization

Although each announcement is unique, depending on the context, they can be classified as three different types:

1. A group announcement in advance informs the employees about an upcoming reorganization involving the loss of several positions.
2. A group announcement with immediate effect informs the employees that an immediate reorganization will occur. This is received as a surprise.
3. An individual announcement informs an employee in an individual meeting that their position will be eliminated.

1. Group announcement in advance

The advance group announcement is the most common approach when the organization is planning a layoff involving a significant number of employees. This type of announcement is handled by the senior management of the company, either in person or electronically, and is generally accompanied by a press release to the media. The language used in the press release is intended to reduce the negative perception pertaining to the upcoming workforce reductions by highlighting the company's new focus and its ability to stand out in a competitive business environment. This kind of announcement can be made many months before the actual changes take place in the company.

Here are a few examples published in newspapers:

- Company X to cut 100 administrative positions. This initiative is intended to reduce operating costs so as to increase flexibility and improve efficiency.
- Each sector of the company reviewed the optimization of our resources and our operations, in order to control

costs. These layoffs will be undertaken as part of healthy daily operations.
- A large corporation announces an upcoming substantial staffing reduction (20,000 jobs) in order to increase its profits and market value.

A group layoff announcement made several months in advance will have psychological impact on the employees. The stress and anxiety caused by impending job insecurity can be devastating, as shown in the previous family analogy. Although in today's workplace, young employees are more mobile and less loyal to their employers, most employees want to keep their current positions for reasons related to financial stability or personal development, or simply because they enjoy their work.

The major drawback of an advance general announcement is the lack of details. How many jobs will be cut? Which departments will be affected? Which criteria will be used for eliminating the positions and reassigning employees? Will seniority be taken into consideration?

The uncertainty is overwhelming. A limited group of decision makers develop the plans for the new structure through an ultra-confidential process. In the meantime, there are many psychological consequences on the employee's health and attitude at work. Based on our experience and testimonials, we identified three types of employees when it comes to dealing with this period of uncertainty and intense stress:

- ✓ the Passives
- ✓ the Chameleons
- ✓ the Anxious

a. The Passive employees (20% of the employees)

During the period of intense stress after the announcement and preceding the actual job cuts, the passives tend to isolate themselves from their colleagues and become unproductive at work. They show up, but that's all, as if they were insensitive to their environment. They act like simple observers in group meetings and avoid taking on any new responsibilities. Some are already looking for new jobs.

b. The Chameleon employees (60% of the employees)

Most employees will act like chameleons, trying to maintain a balanced attitude and avoiding extreme behaviors. These individuals are optimistic by nature and use their emotional intelligence to survive. As a good team player, the chameleon encourages their colleagues, saying that everyone is in the same boat. In such a situation, their mindset is to rally together to help each other face the storm.

c. The Anxious employees (20% of the employees)

The anxious types are at the opposite end of the spectrum from the passive employees. They will manage their stress by increasing their pace at work, to the point of risking burnout. Perfectionists by nature, these individuals will try to take care of every single detail in order to impress their bosses and save their jobs. They will be overly zealous, which also demonstrates a reduction in their self-confidence. There is also a risk of isolation.

Regardless of the category in which they find themselves, all employees build shells to manage the anxiety resulting from the possibility of losing their jobs. Compensatory mechanisms of survivor syndrome, appear as:

- ✓ increased stress, anxiety, insecurity, resilience, cynicism
- ✓ risk aversion when decisions are required
- ✓ distrust of colleagues and managers
- ✓ reduction in teamwork, collaboration is more difficult than during normal times
- ✓ decreased productivity at work, lack of motivation and lack of commitment

In addition to the individual symptoms, the overall work environment becomes heavy and toxic as a result of the rumor mill and uncertainties. All of the testimonials received confirm that a layoff announcement made several months in advance has devastating effects on an employee's personal life and attitude at work. This is one of the most painful situations to be experienced in one's career.

To limit the negative experience of a general group announcement, large companies occasionally specify the division affected by the job cuts. This approach is intended to prevent a loss of productivity on the part of the employees who are not affected. The result is that the company has to deal with two separate groups of employees: the lucky ones, and the unlucky ones. If both groups of employees have to work together on a daily basis, that can result in a toxic work atmosphere. As a result of human nature, the "lucky" employees will feel more important and occasionally more competent than those who do the same kind of work in the unlucky division. Since not all of the employees in the unlucky division will lose their jobs, the relationships between the employees in both groups may become difficult, even abrasive, once the new structure is implemented. Regardless whether the group announcement identifies a particular division or is more general, the devastating consequences are the same for the employees.

2. Group announcement with immediate effect

When the objective is to act quickly, some executives opt to make a group announcement that takes immediate effect. Of course, this creates shock and surprise for employees. In order to fully understand the impact of the unexpected group announcement, let's start with two testimonials.

Ben, a business development representative detailed such a process:

> *One Friday, all of the representatives received a summons for an urgent meeting to be held in a hotel the following Monday, asking them to bring their computers. When they arrived at the hotel, each employee was directed either to Room A or to Room B. Those who went to Room A received a confidential envelope containing the details of their employment termination and were required to hand over their computers, cell phones, and keys for the company cars. The employees in Room B were informed about a reorganization within the company and their new functions as a result.*

Anthony, an accounting clerk, experienced a different method:

> *One morning when I walked into the office, I noticed that there were red and green pieces of cardboard on the chair of each employee in my department. The employees with the green pieces of cardboard kept their jobs and those with the red pieces of cardboard had a few minutes to empty their desks and head for the human resources department.*

In this digital age, reorganization announcements are less and less personalized, more frequently communicated electronically in a detached impersonal manner. Regardless of how the news is delivered, it is easy to imagine the shock that an unexpected announcement represents for the employees who have to leave the company. This shock can be severe, and reverberates throughout all of the survivors. The advantage of this approach is that it serves to prevent the loss of employee productivity that occurs when job cuts are announced a few months in advance. However, the challenge of an announcement with immediate effect is to manage the shock experienced by the employees quickly and effectively. The breach in the bond of trust between the employer and the employees has to be managed immediately. In these situations, all survivors expect to receive clear explanations of the goals pursued by the reorganization and changes in their responsibilities and work environment. But above all, these survivors need reassurance and encouragement, because, based on their most recent experience, they know that it could be their turn to lose their job in the next reorganization.

3. Individual announcement

When layoffs impact a limited number of employees, an individual meeting between each employee concerned and his manager is the most respectful approach.

Dalia, an account manager, experienced this type of announcement:

> *One Friday, my boss called to inform me that there would be cuts in our department and that my job could well be cut in the near future. My first reaction was to ask him: can you tell me Yes or No whether my job will be cut. His response was transparent and he said: YES. Moreover, he told me that the company was satisfied with my work, and that if I was prepared to move to another city, I could keep my job. The exact departure date was not specified, but it was supposed to be in four to five weeks. Suddenly, I started to cry, and I cried the entire weekend. What I found most painful was that I wouldn't see my clients again and I would lose my work colleagues. How would they react? I didn't want to leave my "work family" with whom I had worked the past eight years.*
>
> *Monday morning, my sadness went away and I rolled up my sleeves saying, "Well, what's the next step?" I still had a paying job for the next few weeks and I had to determine my priorities. I'm pleased that my boss informed me in advance in order to give me an opportunity to digest the company's decision. My boss*

> *asked me to keep our conversation confidential and not to discuss it with my work colleagues. The advantage of this approach is that I didn't have to manage the double shock of losing my job and the emotional telephone calls from my colleagues at the same time. When the reorganization was announced four weeks later, I was at peace, and I was able to manage my colleagues' shock efficiently. I vented all of the negative feelings with my spouse without involving my colleagues. I felt that it was less humiliating to find out in advance and in a confidential manner.*

An individual meeting or meetings in small groups with the employee(s) impacted by a reorganization serve to limit outbursts of frustration and contamination of all the employees in the company. The key to success lies in the manner in which the announcement is made by the managers and the follow-up with the impacted employees during the period between the confidential meeting and the official announcement.

Limiting the damage caused by the announcement

There is a direct link between the manner in which an announcement of a reorganization involving job losses is made and the reactions of the survivors. Several factors play a key role in how the employees will react:

- ✓ the length of time between the announcement and the date of the layoffs
- ✓ the transparency and authenticity of all communications
- ✓ the state of the bond of trust between the employees and the managers
- ✓ the corporate culture

The time between the decision made by senior management to implement a reorganization involving job cuts and the announcement made to the employees is crucial, because employees may get wind of a reorganization. Bad news travels quickly! The time between the announcement of job cuts and the implementation of the new structure must be as short as possible in order to limit the period of uncertainty. If the number of job losses is minimal, it is preferable to use the individual approach with the employees impacted. A group announcement is necessary when many positions are eliminated across several departments. When a single department is affected, the potential of collateral damage must be recognized in advance, and prevented.

The golden rule under these circumstances is to communicate the information in a transparent manner, explaining the reason behind the decision to eliminate positions without making any reference to the employees' performance. The strength of the bond of trust between the employees and their managers is directly related to the recognition of transparency, honesty, and authenticity of the communications. There must be a climate of mutual respect in all communications. A frequent mistake on the part of managers is to talk only about upcoming changes and forget to mention anything that will not change within the organization. It is part of human nature to have an intrinsic need to be reassured about what will not change in their work environment. Therefore, it is important to highlight the upcoming changes as well as the things that will remain the same.

Hiding the truth from the employees is the worst mistake a manager can make to break the bond of trust.

Charles, an experienced business analyst, expressed the consequences:

> *After surviving five reorganizations, it's easy for me to recognize the signs of an impending storm. I'm a dynamic person who always sees the positive side of situations, but cynicism quickly takes over my daily life as a result of senior management's lack of transparency when it comes time to announce a reorganization. Management should not treat the employees like fools, trumpeting loud and strong that everything is fine when everyone knows that things are going badly. That demonstrates a lack of respect for the employees. It is difficult to maintain a high level of commitment to one's employer under such circumstances.*

There are respectful ways to announce a reorganization that involves job cuts. Unfortunately, too few managers have the training required to manage this type of situation properly. The slightest error can have harmful long-term effects on the work atmosphere and the performance of the company. In the aftermath of the announcements, survivors must immediately be met with individually, the organizational changes and the implications for their daily work and everything that will not change in their tasks and responsibilities must be explained to them. Some successful employees may find themselves unmotivated if they perceive that the company has not made every effort to reduce the number of job losses. It is in the best interest of managers to prepare for all eventualities within their teams once a reorganization has been announced. Let's hope that the preferred approach will be to make the announcement by means of an individual meeting with each impacted employee and their immediate superior whenever possible.

The announcement day

The day has come for management to inform the employees who will be affected by the layoffs. Most companies use a predetermined sequential order with human resources for activating a reorganization process.

Kevin, a team manager, outlined the steps:

> *On Monday morning, an email is sent to all the employees, informing them that a new organizational structure will be implemented over the coming days and that, unfortunately, some employees will have to leave the company. The employees impacted will be contacted for a meeting with a company manager and a human resources representative on Tuesday and Wednesday. Thursday morning, the new managers will be informed about their responsibilities and those of their team members. Thursday afternoon, these managers will contact each member of their new*

> *team to explain their new positions to them. The first meeting of the new team will take place on Friday morning. Out of respect for those who are leaving, there will be no official announcement of their departure. It's a guessing game!*

This is the kind of week that brings a wide range of emotions to the surface. People scramble to understand who was called Monday in order to find out the names of those leaving. Those who were not contacted feel relieved and consider themselves survivors, still having a job. Then, the survivors have to wait a few days to find out the name of their new boss, their new position, and the members of their team. Following that, everyone sets out on a new path, trying to let go of the emotions of the past few days and adapt to their new work environment.

It requires a high level of emotional intelligence to go through such difficult moments calmly. Above all, people have to avoid judging both the people who have left and the survivors. It is important to vent stress and emotions. Loved ones and friends outside the company are the best people to confide in during a crisis situation.

This type of week is also very challenging for managers. The top priority following an announcement is taking care of the employees who are leaving, making sure they are treated with dignity and respect. The employer has legal obligations to respect whenever jobs are cut. Following that, the employer must meet with the survivors and announce the new hierarchical structure.

As a result of the numerous reorganizations in today's business environment, an employee can be a survivor one day and lose their job a few months later.

The following testimonial highlights the state of mind of Cathy, an employee experiencing a job loss:

> *My employer was my second family. After my separation from my spouse, I had to deal with a second separation ... from my employer, my work colleagues, my friends. I had heard rumors about a reorganization. You always hope that your bosses will support you because you've done a good job. I got a call from the vice president's assistant one Friday at about 3:00 p.m. The message was: Human resources wants to meet with you next Monday. Make sure you bring your computer and your cell phone. Don't get stressed out. They just want to meet with you to discuss the reorganization. My first reaction: I was angry, furious, since I felt that they were passing me by after I had given 200% to the company. When you get home, you try to call your contacts, your trusted colleagues, to find out if you're the only one who got such a call. Did I make some unforgivable mistake? Monday morning, I was beside myself, not knowing what to expect. I went into the meeting room and saw an envelope on the table, a box of Kleenex, and a bottle of water. I had a bad feeling about things. I felt like I was in the dock in a courtroom. What are they going to criticize*

> *me for? When you're on the other side of the table, you want things to be brief. After 18 years with the same company, where I had held several positions with increasing responsibilities, I had the shock of my life. My job was cut without any warning. And several of my colleagues suffered the same fate. The result of a corporate reorganization.*

Losing a job is a major emotional shock for any employee who has invested 100% in their work. The feeling of emptiness experienced following the loss of a job is also felt by survivors who are transferred to another department with a new position and a new boss. These survivors who remain with the company sometimes have to start from square one again, with new responsibilities in another department.

This chapter highlighted the acute stress and distress experienced by employees following a reorganization announcement. Such situations provide an opportunity to reflect on our expectations concerning our employer. And for the survivors who find themselves with a new boss or new responsibilities, the tacit boss-employee mutual agreement that takes the place of the psychological contract will have to be renegotiated. We will discuss this in greater detail in the fourth chapter.

Regardless of the type of announcement, the challenge for the management team is to reduce the impact of the earthquake and the state of shock felt by all the employees. Moreover, it is the bond of trust between the employees and senior management that suffers if it is not addressed in advance. The employees' level of commitment could decline drastically if senior leadership does not explain the reasons for its decision clearly, transparently, and sincerely. A climate of distrust quickly develops if the employees believe that jobs were cut without any logical justification or in a way that is not fair. The consequences will have a negative impact on both the work atmosphere and productivity. Several employees will question the pertinence of making additional efforts as a result of the uncertainty of losing their job the next time. If the organizational changes are implemented without consideration for the impact on the employees, it will have a significant negative impact on the company's profits that could well take three to four years to overcome. To support this point, a study has found that, as a result of layoffs, "survivors experienced a 41% decline in job satisfaction, a 36% decline in organizational commitment, and a 20% decline in job performance."[7]

Executive leaders should consider all possible alternatives before making a reorganization announcement. Some companies have developed new approaches to managing workforce transitions and exploring alternatives to layoffs. A recent paper written by Sandra J. Sucher and Shalene Gupta highlighted successful approaches conducted by large organizations like Nokia, AT&T, and Michelin.[8] An interesting finding from their research is that these companies developed workforce change strategies in which employees are trusted to perform well and are considered the most important asset that will provide short-term and long-term shareholder benefits. This approach helped these organizations to successfully manage organizational changes while preserving employees' support and engagement.

---

7. Sandra J. Sucher and Shalene Gupta, "Layoffs that don't break your company," *Harvard Business Review*, Vol. 96, No. 3, (May–June 2018): 122–129.
8. Sandra J. Sucher and Shalene Gupta, "Layoffs that don't break your company," *Harvard Business Review*, Vol. 96, No. 3, (May–June 2018): 122–129.

Unfortunately, too many executives use the excuse of a resource optimization process to conduct layoffs and, therefore, avoid difficult discussions related to employees' performance. In addition, if employees perceive that the reorganization was implemented for strictly short-term financial gains without considering the impact on employees, the consequences will be devastating. Employees need to feel that the process of conducting a reorganization makes sense and is fair for everybody. And if layoffs cannot be avoided, it is critical to minimize the harm they cause. The common theme of all companies that have succeeded in achieving the objectives set by their reorganization has been the active involvement of all employees.

When reality hits

Sarah, a sales representative, journaled the impact of a reorganization announcement on her:

> *I'm familiar with change!* Over the past 15 years, I worked for five different companies. Permanent position, contractual position, reorganization, corporate merger ... I've experienced it all. I'm not afraid of change. I'm a representative and I travel to meet clients. Changing jobs means a lot of things for me: I get to know the promoted products, the territory, the customers, my new team, and my new boss. I also need to learn the corporate procedures, policies, and software to do my work.

In short, I adapt well to change, and I have demonstrated this on several occasions during the course of my career. In fact, I like change because it enables me to get out of my comfort zone, to learn new things, to meet interesting people, to work on projects, etc.

I love my work! *Convincing a client to try my product gives me an incredible amount of satisfaction. I have a great deal of autonomy when it comes to developing projects, and I make the most of this. I enjoy working with my colleagues and collaborating with them is pleasant.*

Groundhog Day. *On a beautiful day in September, a work colleague informed me that she had been summoned by our boss to an urgent confidential meeting at 9 a.m. the next morning. She had not been told the purpose of the meeting. A short while later, another colleague informed me that he too had been summoned to a meeting, this time for 10 a.m. They had both been asked to take their computers with them. That's when I made the connection. Something was going on. I called my boss to learn more, but was unable to reach him. It was a bit like Groundhog Day: the employees were sent out naked to face the storm while the bosses hid in their dens.*

I'm furious! *I'm still in shock over the fact that they butchered our five-person team and two of my* *colleagues lost their jobs. The three remaining employees have to do all the work now. No empathy on the part of my bosses. It is understood that they believe we should consider ourselves lucky for still having jobs ... as if we had won the lottery. What a joke! What upsets me the most is their hypocrisy. They've cut our personnel by 40% and just six months ago they reassured us that our jobs with the company were secure. A business decision to reduce expenses!*

I'm unable to work and feel like a zombie. *I turn up for work, but nothing more. I only reply to urgent emails. My boss called me to discuss my new responsibilities and I listened to him without reacting. The two colleagues I really enjoyed working with lost their jobs and that affected me as much as if I had lost my own job. I feel a void around me. I've lost my benchmarks. Everything is frozen. We don't have fun anymore. No empathy on the part of the bosses. It's as if they don't understand what I'm going through. I feel like a sticky note on their organization chart. A sticky note that can be crumpled up and thrown away at any time. I no longer trust my boss. Too many situations in which the truth has been hidden and promises have been forgotten. I can't listen to their lies anymore.*

For two months now, I've been standing still. *The flavor of my job has changed. I do the strict minimum just to keep my job. The crack in our team has grown* into a chasm. One of my colleagues decided to adopt a "corporate" attitude the day after the reorganization. He pays no attention to the lies spread by the bosses. At the same time, he's bowing to their every whim to get a promotion. I don't recognize him anymore, he's changed so much. It's discouraging because I can't trust him anymore. We no longer talk to one another, except when necessary.

I am demotivated. The job cuts have had an impact on other departments. A large cloud has formed over our heads. It's crazy how things changed overnight. We're walking on eggshells. We're afraid of making mistakes. We've lost our enthusiasm. Everyone does their own thing without speaking to the others. Team spirit has evaporated. Collaboration has decreased to what is strictly necessary. I no longer feel like working, although I like my work. Given the additional workload, I'm going to have to work overtime. Goodbye quality of life.

I feel caught in a trap. Within hours after the jobs were cut, I received a message from my boss: contacting the colleagues who lost their jobs was forbidden. As if those people had suddenly caught the plague and were "personae non gratae." Hey, those people are my friends! I can't ignore them, particularly when they need help. And in professional terms, transferring files is impossible. So, I have to start over at zero with the *clients that my colleagues visited. What a mess! It will take time for me to become efficient with the addition of these new responsibilities. I feel like I've been left all on my own, with no resources and no support for managing the extra workload. What's the point in making additional efforts if my boss doesn't acknowledge them?*

I don't recognize myself. *My sleep is disrupted. I have no patience. I feel frustrated. I'm becoming cynical. I've always performed well and demonstrated leadership. What's happening? I've lost my motivation. I no longer feel like going to work.*

TO SUMMARIZE

Any reorganization announcement creates tremendous stress for all employees and their families. There are numerous consequences: changes of attitude at work, loss of motivation, vacation plans postponed, and financial uncertainty, to name a few. There are solutions for reducing this stress, with regards to the way the announcement will be made and how it will be managed afterward. Managers need to demonstrate strong emotional intelligence skills to manage departures and to take care of survivors.

Our suggestion is to use a transparent approach to explain the objectives of the reorganization. **Explain what will change and what will not change within the organization.** A confidential discussion to reassure an employee will have a significant impact on reducing anxiety, maintaining motivation, and preserving mutual employee-boss trust. A winning strategy is a development plan for employees at risk of being affected by organizational change to help them acquire new skills to preserve their jobs.

Chapter 2

SURVIVORS OF A REORGANIZATION

Who are the survivors? Who is likely to experience the symptoms of survivor syndrome? Do you have colleagues at work who unknowingly act like survivors? Our discussions with employees and managers who have experienced reorganizations have led to a common conclusion: corporate managers tend to underestimate the impact a reorganization has on the behaviors of survivors. This is largely because most employees and managers have a very limited knowledge of the behaviors related to survivor syndrome. These behaviors will be discussed in this chapter.

For starters, all of the employees who remain with a company following a reorganization involving job losses are considered survivors. Managers and directors can also develop survivor behaviors; no one is spared. There are even collateral effects on the departments that were not affected by job losses. For example, job cuts in the computer support (IT) department will have an impact on the other departments since the employees are used to collaborating.

Here, coauthor Nicole Labbe shares her own experience as a survivor of several reorganizations:

> *On an emotional level, each reorganization represented a new challenge with its batch of surprises. On top of the change management adjustments, the uncertainty of losing your own job generates an additional stress in this already challenging environment.*
>
> *Looking back, I realize that I experienced several symptoms of survivor syndrome, without realizing it. At work, the professional image of the leader was predominant since I had to show that I was steadfast, confident, serene and positive. Back at home, I realized that I was stressed out, frustrated, and tired. I believed that I was the only one in the company experiencing this situation. The most difficult reorganization was the one in which the job cuts were announced several months in advance. I worked more than six months without knowing if I would keep my job or lose it at the end of the year. The work atmosphere was very heavy. Several employees did their work without interacting with the others. Certain departments worked in silos and cooperation was difficult. The rumor mill was operating at full speed. Important decisions were postponed. Many departments were managed in "zero risk" mode because we were all afraid of making mistakes. We all felt that the slightest error or negative attitude increased our chances of losing our job.*

The day of the announcement, I was relieved and happy to be keeping my job, but sad for my colleagues who had left. I felt that some of the decisions were unjust for the employees affected. I had to manage my emotions as a survivor of the reorganization, master my new responsibilities, and get to know my new boss, while assuming leadership of a new team of surviving employees.

In the weeks following one particular reorganization, I totally lost confidence in my skills. I was an experienced and high-performing manager, and yet I felt isolated, incompetent, unmotivated, and unable to deal with challenges. My boss was overwhelmed and I did not feel that my work was appreciated. At the same time, I had employees who were finding it hard to deal with the stress of the reorganization, and I realized that listening to them and trying to encourage them was draining my energy. These employees had also lost their self-esteem and were afraid of making mistakes. I needed a vacation, but the timing wasn't right. I wasn't able to see the light at the end of the tunnel as a result of the additional work. I was working every evening and occasionally on weekends, and yet I wasn't being paid for overtime. I was in survival mode and close to burning out.

All reorganizations are unique for both the company and the employees concerned. And each individual reacts to this stress in a different manner.

"Whoa ... I was afraid, but I'm happy to keep my job." That's the immediate reaction of most employees when they learn that they won't be losing their job. It's an intense reaction of relief and a temporary release of the stress accumulated. There's also a sensation of emptiness: where have I landed, who else has landed with me, who will my new colleagues be? My new boss? My new responsibilities?

The initial feeling of euphoria at having kept your job is followed by a period of grieving. Grieving for your former position and for your colleagues and friends who have left the company. Once back at work, new sources of stress arise as the employee must adapt quickly and perform in their new role while working to earn the trust of their new boss and the new team. Following this, the symptoms of survivor syndrome will appear in an insidious manner. There is a desire to start over again, but the body is not on the same wavelength. Energy and enthusiasm are frequently lacking. As proud warriors, we tell ourselves that things will pass, that it's just a difficult period that we have to get through and that, above all, the timing is not good since the company is going through a transformation. Survivor syndrome sets in.

What is survivor syndrome?

The term "survivor's syndrome" (now known more commonly as "survivor syndrome") originated during World War II when researchers conducted studies on the symptoms of soldiers and Holocaust survivors who had experienced traumatic situations.

One survivor may have the impression that he is not entitled to feel bad since he is still alive. Yet, his suffering is real; the symptoms of this syndrome include traumatic shock, a feeling of guilt, and anxiety.

The expression "survivor syndrome" is also used to describe the behaviors and emotions of the employees who remain with a company following a reorganization involving job cuts. Several studies have been published on the topic and the references are provided in the appendix.[9] Despite this, **most company managers ignore the symptoms of survivor syndrome because they have not been trained to recognize or address them.** This lack of recognition should be of corporate concern, since 80% of companies do not attain their objectives following a major reorganization.[10] Company managers tend to underestimate the costs resulting from the drop in their employees' productivity, the exhaustion resulting from the additional workload, and the loss of skills and organizational memory. A better understanding of survivor syndrome will be beneficial for both managers and employees.

Companies often invest considerable sums to provide assistance to the employees who leave the company. The terminated employees have access to psychological assistance provided by professionals, career counselling, self-help groups, etc. It is important to help the employees who leave, and these services are greatly appreciated.

But what is done for the employees who remain with the organization? Generally, nothing. The survivors are considered lucky to have kept their jobs. Managers make a serious mistake when they

---

9. Amy J. Kupec, "Overcoming the survivor's syndrome: Current theories and practices" (master's thesis, DePaul, 2010), 67, https://via.library.depaul.edu/etd/67/
10. S. Heidari Robinson and S Heywood, "Getting Reorgs Right," *Harvard Business Review*, Vol. 94, No. 11, (November 2016): 84–89.

ignore the psychological impacts of a reorganization. It is unrealistic for any employee to return to work the following morning with a "business as usual" attitude, as if nothing had happened.

Kyle, a manager of a large retail company said:

> *I lost several very competent colleagues in recent years following reorganizations. These colleagues found new jobs with companies that are growing. For my part, the work environment is difficult and depressing, since we are declining. The big winners following reorganizations are not necessarily those who stay with the company.*

The surviving employees know full well that they are considered "privileged," and this feeling is encouraged and reinforced by senior management, which wants to motivate its troops. Suffering from survivor syndrome is sometimes perceived as a weakness, and each employee or manager will do everything possible to hide what they are dealing with in the aftermath: anxiety, uncertainty, stress, sleeping difficulties, frustration, fatigue, etc. People voluntarily ignore their problems, telling themselves that they are fleeting. They are afraid of sharing their emotions and problems, since this could be interpreted as difficulty adapting to the change. People shouldn't kid themselves, all employees and managers, regardless of their hierarchical level, are at risk of suffering from survivor syndrome. Most of them live in denial, but the symptoms are present. This is a taboo subject that needs to be demystified, since reorganizations and job cuts are now part of today's workplace reality.

Recognizing survivor syndrome

Survivor syndrome encompasses numerous behaviors and emotions. Each employee reacts differently, depending on their personality, psychological state, and financial and family situation. Researchers Mishra et al. identified four archetypes of survivor responses following a downsizing.[11]

1. The **"active advocates"** have a constructive and positive attitude and demonstrate initiative and leadership.
2. The **"faithful followers"** have an attitude of respect toward the changes, without necessarily accepting them. They remain loyal to the company. They are passive, doing only what they are asked to do and nothing more.
3. The **"walking wounded"** are fearful and follow instructions out of fear of reprisals. They tend to isolate themselves.
4. The **"carping critics"** have a negative attitude. They express anger and cynicism toward the organization.

How does a survivor fall into one category rather than another? According to these researchers, the key factors that will influence the employee's behavior are the bond of trust with management and the feeling of empowerment in doing his job. Survivors who have a low level of trust in management and who feel disempowered will develop a fearful attitude like that of a walking wounded. On the other end of the spectrum, an employee who has a high

---

[11]. Aneil K. Mishra et al. "Downsizing the company without downsizing morale," MIT *Sloan Management Review*, (Spring 2009): 41. www.sloanreview.mit.edu.

level of trust in his superior along with a strong feeling of empowerment at work could become an active advocate.[12]

It is possible to reduce the effects of survivor syndrome in the aftermath of a reorganization. It all depends on the attitude of the manager and the employee. The two key ingredients for success are:

- *Trust*: To build a relationship of mutual trust between employee and manager that is transparent, authentic and respectful
- *Empowerment*: To ensure a work environment where everyone has the autonomy to assume leadership in the performance of their tasks and responsibilities

Regardless of the type of survivor response, some behaviors or emotions can be expressed to varying degrees. They may appear in the days following the reorganization, or even several months later. Research has demonstrated that some employees continue to experience symptoms five years after the event.[13]

The first behavior to appear is often denial. Denegation acts somewhat like a shock absorber following a reorganization to allow the employee to develop their own defense mechanisms. Refusal to see reality, unawareness of the symptoms of anxiety, repression of emotions, isolation, and desire to project a positive image are all examples of denial. Every excuse for denial is acceptable. Acknowledging the existence of denial is the first step in initiating personal soul-searching into one's physical and mental state.

---

12. Ibid.
13. David M. Noer, *Healing the Wounds,* (San Francisco: Jossey-Bass, 1993), 71.

Manifestations of survivor syndrome

The emotions and behaviors related to survivor syndrome have been described abundantly in the literature. We have decided to arrange them in two categories in order to facilitate personal reflection:

1. Personal manifestations
2. Impacts on the employee's work

As a general rule, the first behaviors to appear in survivors are personal in nature. The manner in which these emotions and behaviors are managed will have a direct impact on attitudes at work. If you have survived a reorganization, we suggest you read this list slowly, taking the time to reflect and do some soul-searching about each emotion or behavior. Don't hesitate to consult people who know you well for their perspectives and opinions, as they might have observed changes in your attitude.

SURVIVOR SYNDROME — **Personal manifestations**

Immediate feeling of relief (when you learn that you keep your job)
Stress, anxiety, fatigue, sleeping difficulties
Feeling of injustice, betrayal, sadness
Frustration, impatience
Feeling of insecurity, guilt, lack of motivation
Loss of self-confidence, personal questioning, loss of confidence in your future with the company
Feeling alone, isolated, withdrawing
Difficulty managing one's emotions, fear of sharing emotions with others
Sense of loss of control
Attitude of denial, refusal to see reality as it is, tendency to form a shell and ignore your suffering
Fear or nervousness that your work is not recognized or appreciated

SURVIVOR SYNDROME — Impacts on the employee's work

Negative attitude, cynicism
Difficulty concentrating, focusing
Loss of productivity
Dissatisfaction and frustration with respect to leadership
Loss of trust in the company, its values, its culture
Working in a silo, reducing cooperation and sharing of information
Lack of commitment to work, reluctance to get involved in new projects
Absence of leadership
Higher tolerance of previously considered unacceptable things
Tendency to blame others, managers, competitors
Need to be informed about everything, about the company's direction, and rumors
Difficulty setting priorities, loss of control related to work overload
Risk aversion when making decisions, prefer the status quo
Reduction in creativity, no wish to take the initiative

Experiencing a reorganization that entails job cuts is stressful. This stress takes a different form, but is not completely eliminated, when the employee's position is confirmed. The anxiety involved when you expect you are about to lose your job will always be present to various degrees. There is also the stress caused by the new position, duties, and responsibilities. Interpersonal relations could become another source of stress for some people when it comes to adapting to the requirements of the new boss and developing cooperative relationships with new work colleagues.

Adam, an engineer, admitted:

> *I'm a passionate person who likes to give 100% at work. After each reorganization, I continued working without feeling that I was starting over again. I was motivated and I felt in control of the situation. I wanted to show that I was a leader who adapted easily to change. It was much later that I started to experience a few subtle symptoms. I felt more tired and less motivated when it came to performing the tasks involved in my job. I felt overwhelmed by the workload, but I told myself that it was only temporary and I would catch up over time. I refused to acknowledge that I was exhausted until I found myself on sick leave and was forced to face up to the situation. No one had ever mentioned survivor syndrome to me. I always adapted well to change, but I realized that the stress involved in a reorganization can be insidious.*

Blinded by his emotions and his desire to succeed, this survivor was close to burnout by ignoring his symptoms. This denial is easy to understand when you remember that a survivor is considered a privileged person within their personal and professional environment, since they did not lose their job.

Hannah, a logistic coordinator, described the pervasive symptoms:

> *In the weeks following the reorganization, I lost count of how many colleagues came to my office to let off steam, vent, and even weep. The stress accumulated before and after the reorganization became more and more difficult to bear.*

There were many causes for distress, but the reasons most often given to Hannah can be categorized according to four major themes:

1. The feeling of being left on one's own, without any support
2. The additional workload without the possibility of seeing the light at the end of the tunnel
3. The lack of communication with the employee's immediate superior combined with the feeling that the additional efforts made were not being recognized and appreciated
4. The disarray caused by the inability to find solutions to improve the situation

All of these employees experienced symptoms of survivor syndrome without realizing it. No one had heard about survivor syndrome. And yet, the suffering was quite real. Hannah's testimonial illustrates the difficulties experienced following a reorganization in a context in which the managers do not take the time to listen and acknowledge their employees. It is true that employees find it easier to confide in a colleague than in their superior. For this reason, it is important to inform managers and employees about the various aspects of survivor syndrome so as to reduce the impact.

Employee loyalty following a reorganization

An employee's loyalty is related directly to the level of employee-employer trust. Can the employees trust their employer to offer them stimulating jobs and develop their competencies? Will my efforts be acknowledged appropriately? Will my boss support me if I make a mistake? Does my boss trust me? Can I trust my boss?

If the trust relationship is fragile or nonexistent, the employees will grow disillusioned. This disillusionment is the result of a loss of confidence in the company managers and is accompanied by a sense of betrayal and frustration. The employees' commitment to their work declines. The employees do what they are asked to do, but nothing more. Creativity and innovation are lacking, since the employees are afraid to make mistakes and take risks. They prefer the status quo to making a decision that involves risk. The additional work will make it difficult to establish priorities, resulting in additional stress. The employees are hesitant to express their problems out of fear of reprisals and of being viewed as finding it difficult to adapt to change. A climate of suspicion and mistrust may settle in. This all has a direct impact on cooperation and teamwork.

"Once bitten, twice shy." This saying provides an apt description of survivors who become more cautious when making decisions and even develop a sense of distrust concerning their employer. Every survivor will experience emotions following a reorganization. For some, it is an emotional wound that is difficult to forget and haunts them, depending on the circumstances. The survivor who is dissatisfied with their new position or new team can become a "wounded follower," despite their initial positive attitude.

Impact of a demotion

An organizational change can affect the hierarchy level of a few employees. Some of them may be promoted, while others will be demoted to a lower level with reduced responsibilities. In the context of a demotion, the employee still has a job, but there are no longer any new challenges. Several questions will come to torment this employee: *What will my colleagues think? Will my immediate superior recognize my skills? Has my career come to an end? How do I motivate myself?* An ambitious person who no longer has the opportunity for advancement as a result of a reorganization may also be faced with this same dilemma. Does this mean promotions are no longer possible? The employee feels diminished, or "shelved." Many people who have experienced this situation say it takes additional time to heal from the demotion. It is a direct affront to one's ego and one's self-esteem.

In sectors that are growing, the employee can leave their position to work for another company—but what happens when the competitors are not hiring? The survivor has a difficult decision to make:

- ✓ keep his job, keep his head down, and put up with things in the hope that the situation will improve
- ✓ keep his job and focus his energy on a personal project that will provide a great deal of satisfaction outside of work
- ✓ leave his job to make a career change

✓ leave his job and take the time to find a satisfactory job even if it takes some time

There is no easy choice. Refusing to act will lead to burnout. Even worse, the reputation of this once-performing employee will be negatively affected. The demoted employee has to act and make a decision, since the status quo is only viable on a medium-term basis.

Lindsey, a finance manager, describes the dilemma:

> *The demotion was a painful challenge for me. It was a hard pill to swallow. On the one hand, the company told me that they appreciated me as an employee and wanted to keep me. On the other hand, they offered me a position that represented a major step backwards in my career path. It was as if the company didn't know what to do with me. I needed a few days to think about things and weigh the pros and cons of the proposal. In my mind, I had three options:*
>
> 1. *I quit my job and I look for a new one elsewhere;*
> 2. *I play the hand that was dealt to me up to the point that I will no longer be able to tolerate it;*
> 3. *I accept the demotion and work hard and get a promotion in the near future.*

In the case of a demotion, the soundness of the employee-employer trust relationship is strained, and will be a determining factor in the employee's decision to remain with the company.

Managing stress

A reorganization involving job losses is in itself a situation that generates acute stress for both employees and managers. An employee for a large company related that he worked with several colleagues who found it very difficult to survive reorganizations. These colleagues displayed negative attitudes toward the company, their colleagues, and their responsibilities. They viewed the reorganization as a fatality. They had doubts, wondering why they should work harder if they were going to lose their jobs in six months anyway. They programmed themselves to be negative. They blamed others; everything was someone else's fault. They realized that they weren't the most competent at their work, but did nothing to correct their shortcomings or even ask for help. After a while, they intentionally cut ties with their colleagues and isolated themselves.

The employees who experience difficulties adapting to their new work environment, or who develop a negative attitude, are not bad people. Far from it. As a general rule, these employees performed well before the reorganization. How can their descent into disinterest and negativity be explained? One thing is obvious: they are no longer happy at work. The answer may lie in the way they manage their stress.

Researchers in the field of neuroscience now have a better understanding of the mechanisms that affect individuals' responses to stress. Each situation is unique: a person may not be affected by a stress present in situation X and yet react negatively to the stress of situation Y. A stressful situation such as the announcement of a reorganization could provoke a variety of reactions on the part of the individuals concerned. In short, we never know how we will react, but there are tools to help us deal with stressful situations and manage them effectively so as to limit the damage.

Stress as such is not always negative. Quite the contrary. We all need stress to live and to deal with the threats in our environment. Acute stress increases vigilance and allows us to delve into our energy in order to deal with a threat or an unexpected situation. A well-managed stressful situation allows us to move out of our comfort zone, face new challenges, and perform. This stress has a positive impact on self-esteem, since we are proud of our success. In the case of a reorganization, each individual will interpret this situation of acute stress in a different manner. Some will turn the page quickly without consequences, while other employees will develop chronic stress that will affect their physical and mental health.

The excellent book *Well Stressed: Manage Stress Before it Turns Toxic*,[14] written by Sonia Lupien, Ph.D., Director of the Center for Studies on Human Stress in Montreal, inspired us to better understand the impact of stress on individuals who survive a reorganization. Her research into human stress taught her that "stress is not an illness, and hence cannot be cured. Stress is a necessary reaction by the body, one that enables us to survive."[15] It is possible to manage our stress, to recognize and understand it, and then develop a resistance that will enable us to deal with unforeseeable situations and threats to our ego and our self-esteem in a healthy manner.

Researchers have demonstrated that a situation must include one of the four following characteristics in order to provoke a stress response:[16]

---

14. Sonia Lupien, *Well Stressed: Manage Stress Before it Turns Toxic* (HarperCollins e-books, Toronto, 2012).
15. Sonia Lupien, *Well Stressed: Manage Stress Before it Turns Toxic* (HarperCollins e-books, Toronto, 2012), 2.
16. Sonia Lupien, "Deconstructing and Reconstructing Stress," *Mammoth Magazine*, no. 16, (Autumn 2016): 3, www.humanstress.ca.

1. **N**ovelty: something new that you have not experienced before
2. **U**npredictability: Something you had no way of knowing it would occur
3. **T**hreat to the ego: Your competence as a person is called into question
4. **S**ense of control: You feel you have little or no control over the situation.

These characteristics form the acronym N.U.T.S., which you will find in the literature on stress.

Someone who survives a reorganization is vulnerable when it comes to dealing with stress, since they have no control over the situation. And the uncertainty about the possibility of losing their job can threaten their ego and self-esteem. If the survivor is given new responsibilities, there will be unexpected situations that may cause a stress reaction. How can the individual deal with this? Initially, the person must do some soul-searching in order to determine the source of the stress. What thoughts haunt you night and day? Those are your stressors!

Dr. Lupien suggests that in order to reduce stress, you must deconstruct the stressful situation, questioning the four aspects of N.U.T.S.:

Is it a new situation?
Is the situation unpredictable?
Is my ego threatened?
Do I have control over the situation?

Your responses to these questions will help you identify alternatives and solutions for defusing the situation that is the source of your stress, and then develop techniques for coping with it, understanding it, and managing it. The goal is to be able to identify solutions that will stop your ego from feeling threatened, and enable you to take control of the situation. It is not possible to eliminate all stressful situations, but you can learn to manage them differently and avoid suffering. A simple "impression" of having better control over the situation reduces stress significantly.

Some people may say that all this is easier said than done, and we understand that. However, it costs nothing to try! The advantage of this approach is that it addresses the problem at the source instead of avoiding it. Dr. Lupien provides a good example to illustrate her approach. If a work colleague exasperates you, going to the spa on the weekend will not help you solve the problem. It will still be there when you go back to work on Monday. Contrary to popular belief, the opposite of stress is not relaxation, it's resilience. According to Lupien, "Resilience is the ability to have a plan B, a plan C, a plan D, etc. in order to face the situation that stresses you out."[17]

Becoming resilient

It's not possible to talk about survivor syndrome without discussing the notion of resilience. According to human stress researchers, "When facing adversity, being able to positively adapt represents resilience."[18] Resilience is a synonym of flexibility, and is the ability to adapt to a specific stressful situation. When facing a stressful

---

17. Ibid.
18. Oliver Bourdon, "Resilience: When Hope Becomes Possible for Everyone," *Mammoth Magazine*, no. 13 (Summer 2013): 2, www.humanstress.ca.

situation such as a reorganization, the resilient person will adapt positively and get back on their feet quickly.

How can you become resilient? No one is born resilient. You become resilient by working relentlessly to overcome the many obstacles of a challenge. Resilience can be compared to a muscle that can be developed and used as needed.[19] The efforts required to become resilient are personal, and vary from one individual to another.

Researchers in the field of neuroscience have identified several protective factors that help an individual preserve a good psychological and physical balance.[20] Here is a list of some of them:

- ✓ make a positive reappraisal of the situation that generates a great deal of stress
- ✓ have satisfactory social support from family and friends
- ✓ be optimistic
- ✓ give meaning to adversity
- ✓ have a Plan B
- ✓ accept negative emotions and experience them fully without avoiding them
- ✓ take part in an activity you like once this time has passed
- ✓ find personal worth in altruism or volunteering
- ✓ have a positive self-image
- ✓ separate your roles at work, at home or in other spheres of your life

---

19. Sheryl Sandberg and Adam Grant, *Option B: Facing Adversity, Building Resilience, and Finding Joy* (New York: Alfred A. Knopf 2017).
20. Alexandra Bisson-Desrochers, "Protective Factors and Our Resilience Toolbox," *Mammoth Magazine*, no. 13, (Summer 2013): 10, www.humanstress.ca.

Survivors of reorganizations who have developed resilience are those with the best capacity to adapt to change. People with a "chameleon" type personality, as described in the previous chapter, seem to be less affected by reorganizations. They have a positive attitude and an above-average emotional intelligence. They will avoid getting stressed out over things they cannot control. They will absorb shocks and turn the page to start over again. These people have a balanced lifestyle and take the time to eliminate their stress on a daily basis through activities that are beneficial for them. They are resilient. **When they face a stressful situation, they will ask the following question: is this a traumatizing event or a learning opportunity? It's all a matter of perspective!**

When resilience unravels

Coauthor Nicole Labbe recounts having known several people who were models of resilience following multiple reorganizations. These employees continued to be enthusiastic at work, demonstrated leadership, and were not afraid to take the initiative. These same employees and managers, encountered again several years later, demonstrated attitudes that had changed. Outward appearances seemed normal, as they were still dedicated to their work and their behavior was professional. However, the flame that once burned in them and drove them to move heaven and earth for the benefit of the company had gone out. The corporate pride tattoo had faded:

- These employees no longer questioned doubtful decisions. Without discussion, they accepted new procedures that slowed their productivity and even went counter to their department's objectives.

- Unacceptable situations were tolerated. They avoided all conflict and refused to question managers about decisions that could have been improved. They submitted to the managers' wishes without reacting. They adopted a subconscious attitude of withdrawal during meetings. They were physically present at work, but no longer felt concerned about the organization's priorities.

- They were emotionally detached from their responsibilities, their colleagues, and their bosses.

- Gradually, they developed an attitude of disengagement with respect to their work and their employer. They became robots, zombies, technocrats.

Why did this happen? To keep their jobs! This situation is regrettable, but occurs all too frequently in companies and public sector administrations following reorganizations.

Workplace disengagement

In a post-reorganization environment, the implemented and continuous changes are challenging for the employees, making it a critical time for their engagement. The literature on this topic converges toward the same observation: **the factors that promote**

disengagement or demotivation of employees at work are directly related to the bosses' behaviors and leadership styles.[21, 22]

Here are a few examples of behaviors that could lead to employee disengagement. A manager who endorses and accepts an unacceptable situation encourages, through his attitude and behavior, his employees to act in the same manner. A director who does not demonstrate the leadership required for his position will have a negative effect on his subordinates, and the situation will deteriorate when employees perceive that they are not fairly treated. A team leader who demonstrates an attitude of submission and avoids questioning his superiors following a questionable decision will not encourage his employees to demonstrate leadership. A boss who does not speak to his employees, who ignores their emails, who does not acknowledge the work done, will wind up with employees who are unmotivated and uncommitted. A manager who makes promises without following up will lose his employees' respect. A leader who does not advocate for his team or is perceived to be politicizing for his own benefit, will rapidly lose the trust of his employees. It's somewhat like an infection that is transmitted progressively and spreads throughout the entire work team, the department, and the culture of the organization. **When mediocrity is tolerated, it turns into a gangrene that insidiously eats away at each human being—with devastating consequences at all levels.**

---

21. Marco Nink and Jennifer Robinson, "Can Bad Managers Be Saved?" Gallup (December 21, 2016), www.news.gallup.com.
22. Jim Harter, "Dismal Employee Management is a Sign of Global Mismanagement," Gallup (December 20, 2017), http://news.gallup.com.

We have heard several testimonials on this topic from employees experiencing a situation of disengagement at work. Why did they give up and lose their sense of commitment as employees?

Heather, an administrative assistant working for a large organization described how the process overtook her:

> *I gradually lost my interest when we stopped having fun at work. In the past, we worked hard, but we also took the time to laugh. Today, I do the absolute minimum and I'm eager to leave the office at the end of the day.*

Heather's example is indicative of the atmosphere within a department that has deteriorated and become impersonal due to the lack of leadership by the director. Heather said she has always loved her job, and did a lot of work in the office after the reorganization, staying for long hours to help the company achieve their goals. When she realized that her ideas and efforts were no longer being considered, she dropped out. She has become an automaton doing what she is asked to do, and no more.

Robin, a nurse working in a hospital, had a similar experience of alienation:

> *My boss has more than fifty employees under his direct supervision. I never see him because he's always in meetings. I feel abandoned. I no longer get feedback*

> *about my work. We no longer get a little pat on the back to encourage us. Everything has become impersonal. The training new employees receive is minimal and incomplete. There's no one to help them when they make mistakes. I lost interest when I realized that I can't do anything to improve the situation.*

Some of the key factors from these two testimonials that explain how these resilient, committed, and successful employees have stalled and gradually developed an attitude of disengagement toward their work are:

- ✓ lack of support and recognition of efforts
- ✓ lack of dialogue with and advocacy from their boss
- ✓ feeling of not being able to improve the team's productivity
- ✓ development of an impersonal atmosphere

Dealing with disengagement

Any positive impact a company hopes to generate from the reorganization will be nullified if the employees become disengaged. How to define employee engagement? "The concept of employee engagement is sometimes confused with happiness. It's really about an employee's psychological investment in their organization and motivation to produce extraordinary results."[23] It also refers to

---

23. Trends in Global Employee Engagement, (Aon, 2018), www.aon.com.

attitudes which "cluster around consistent themes, such as a clear sense of purpose, a commonly held notion of what's valuable or important, feelings of psychological safety, and confidence about the future."[24]

Statistics concerning employee commitment at work provide food for thought. American polling firm Gallup is renowned in this area. It has been noted that, in North America, only 30% of employees are committed to their work, while 52% are partially disengaged and 18% are actively disengaged.[25] The cost generated by the reduced productivity of employees who are not engaged and are dissatisfied but showing up, is estimated to be between $450 and $550 billion per year.[26] This situation, presenteeism, has a direct impact on the physical and mental health of employees as well as on their attitude at work.

How to recognize these employees? The committed employee is easy to recognize. He is engaged at work and feels useful and appreciated. He shares the vision and goals of the company to become an ambassador. This employee is enthusiastic; he works well with colleagues and has a positive impact on them. This employee demonstrates leadership, problem solving abilities, innovation, and dedication to improve the efficiency of his work environment. Moreover, this employee is very open to feedback and is willing to learn new skills.

At the other extreme, the employee who is actively disengaged is indifferent to their work. This employee has developed an attitude

---

24. Marcus Buckingham and Ashley Goodall, "The Power of Hidden Teams," *Harvard Business Review* (May 2019): https://hbr.org/cover-story/2019/05/the-power-of-hidden-teams.
25. Susan Sorenson and Keri Garman, "How to Tackle U.S. Employees' Stagnating Engagement," *Gallup Business Journal* (June 11 2013,): www.news.gallup.com.
26. Ibid.

of distrust with respect to the organization and management. He is physically present at work, but completely unmotivated. His negative attitude and poor performance with respect to accomplishing his tasks have a detrimental effect on colleagues. This employee wastes time on all sorts of activities that are not related to his responsibilities, such as surfing the Internet in order to avoid doing his own work.[27]

Identifying the employees who make up the 52% group that is partially disengaged is more complex. The behaviors of these employees are subtler, and vary significantly from one individual to another. Their passiveness seems discreet. They are no longer passionate about their work. Their leadership and initiative and the quality of their work is just satisfactory enough to avoid arousing their supervisor's suspicions.

Another contribution to the employee engagement research is the ADP Research Institute 2019 study that measured levels of engagement of more than 19,000 workers around the world. Their study reveals that **"only 16% of employees are fully engaged at work, while about 84% are just going through the motions."**[28] Interestingly, these numbers have not varied much over the last forty years. The study goes on to say that senior leaders' approaches to identifying disengagement is flawed. Employee engagement surveys are touted to provide the company important feedback on its practices, but they frequently and indirectly (or directly) put pressure on employees to provide good feedback on the organization. Unfortunately, some surveys are inadequate to address the

---

27. David Mizne, "5 Surprising Signs of a Disengaged Employee," www.15five.com.
28. Marcus Buckingham and Ashley Goodall, "The Power of Hidden Teams," *Harvard Business Review* (May 2019): https://hbr.org/cover-story/2019/05/the-power-of-hidden-teams.

causes of employee disengagement, which is mainly attributed to the poor quality of the supervisors and their lack of leadership. Here are a few examples of how leaders contribute to their employees' disengagement:

- ✓ lack of or insufficient acknowledgment of efforts made and work done well
- ✓ employees left on their own
- ✓ loss of sense of belonging to a team
- ✓ minimal collaboration among colleagues
- ✓ centralization of decision-making that leads to a lack of accountability and buy-in on the part of the employees
- ✓ limited learning opportunities or challenges for the employees
- ✓ loss of advocacy for your team

So, what can be done to change the attitude of employees who have become disengaged? Strategies for improving employee commitment are generally initiated by management and team leaders. According to the ADP Research Institute, the most effective levers to pull are teamwork and improving team experiences.[29] Employees need to feel part of a team where their efforts and strengths are recognized and valued. There is only one way to create the best team: ensure the team leader is equipped to build trust and give attention to all members in a way that each one is confident and empowered to contribute to the team success. In order to build employee engagement, the team leader should focus on the following actions:

---

29. Marcus Buckingham and Ashley Goodall, "The Power of Hidden Teams," *Harvard Business Review* (May 2019): https://hbr.org/cover-story/2019/05/the-power-of-hidden-teams.

- ✓ creating a work environment in which open and transparent communication is valued
- ✓ providing frequent attention to the work of each team member
- ✓ discussing mutual employer-employee expectations
- ✓ using a personalized approach to identify the strengths of each employee and develop them by offering employees stimulating challenges or development opportunities
- ✓ establishing clear and attainable objectives for each employee and for the team
- ✓ acknowledging efforts and celebrating victories
- ✓ delegating responsibilities to encourage leadership, empowerment, initiative and creativity
- ✓ being an advocate for your team

The leadership team has to acknowledge that the atmosphere at work is no longer the same following a reorganization. This situation of acute stress affects all of the employees, including the managers. And recovery takes several months, maybe even several years if it is not addressed up-front. The risk of having employees who are developing an attitude of disengagement is enormous. An employee who was very motivated and committed before the reorganization can quickly become disengaged against his will. The management team plays a key role in motivating employees and providing a work environment in which each individual feels appreciated. Managers are the ones who pull the strings to avoid the disengagement of their employees. We will discuss the additional skills required by a team leader during a reorganization in the next chapter.

TO SUMMARIZE

The behaviors related to survivor syndrome have many aspects and manifestations. It is much more than "simple" grieving for the employees who have left the company. The impacts on a personal level and at work are considerable and far too often underestimated and ignored. This goes well beyond a problem of adaptation to change; the acute stress caused by the prospect of losing one's job profoundly disrupts employees and team leaders, and can continue, start, or evolve well after the actual reorganization.

How can the impact of survivor syndrome be minimized? A workshop given by a guest speaker on motivation will not solve the problems. Our professional experience combined with the testimonials collected reveal the same thing: **survivor syndrome must be expected, recognized, and discussed openly within the company**. All employees and managers should be familiar with its symptoms and resulting behaviors. Suffering from survivor syndrome is not a conscious and voluntary decision. It's not pleasant for the employees. It contributes to the development of a work environment that is stressful and demotivating and can lead directly to an attitude of disengagement.

The post-reorganization work environment provides fertile soil for the development of survivor syndrome. Since the behaviors involved in survivor syndrome may still be present five years after a painful reorganization, it is never too late to take action.

Chapter 3

ENSURING THE SUCCESS OF THE TEAM FOLLOWING A REORGANIZATION

There are several types of managers within an organization. The directors hold executive positions and supervise the team leaders. The team leaders, in turn, supervise teams of employees directly. They are often called first-line managers, or mid-level executives, since they ensure liaison between the employees and the directors. This chapter discusses the role of the team leader the day following a reorganization and his impact on the employees. If you are an employee, this chapter will be of just as much interest to you; the solutions proposed are intended for everyone who survives a reorganization.

Over the past fifteen years as a team manager, Nicole Labbe survived seven reorganizations involving job cuts within her department. She could no longer count the number of colleagues who lost their jobs. Following each reorganization, she had a new team of employees to get to know, motivate, and coach, who were all survivors. The day following each reorganization, in order to demonstrate leadership and enthusiasm about starting over again, she had to suppress her emotions while adjusting to the new reality of the work environment.

Team leaders play a key role in the success of an organization. Why? Because they are the first people the employees will turn to for answers to their questions, and for reassurance, encouragement, and information about the company's new vision. They provide inspiration to trust in the future, and they navigate the team to attain the corporate objectives and implement the company's new vision. They are also filters when it comes to using common sense for pragmatically overcoming obstacles. In fact, the term "manager" is outdated; companies or public service organizations need *leaders* at all levels. Several books have been written about the essential leadership skills needed by company executives. I think that these leadership skills apply equally to mid-level managers and team leaders.

Unfortunately, team leaders are often bypassed in the reorganization process, and they are only informed about the changes at the same time as the employees. Yet, they shoulder the heaviest burden the day after the changes to the company's structure are announced, healing wounds and rebuilding a dynamic team. And, in most cases, they do this without any training provided by the company to help them. A reorganization does not end on the day when some employees are terminated and then others start over new the next morning as if nothing had happened. On the contrary, the critical step starts on day one following the reorganization. And it is specifically on day one that all of the leaders with employees to supervise must be well prepared to start work in a healthy and productive work environment.

Over the next few pages, we will discuss the impact of reorganizations on the company's control mechanisms, the skills required of a team leader in the case of a reorganization, and the planning of Day 1 with the team. We will use a simple and practical approach to discuss each topic and offer solutions intended for both team leaders and employees.

Impact of company's control mechanisms

Budget restrictions being the cornerstone of the majority of the reorganizations, it is not surprising that the most frequent backlash is the implementation of control mechanisms to limit expenses. New performance measures are introduced where the employee must increase productivity while having fewer resources at his disposal. In a business environment where every dollar is important, executives must make difficult decisions, and the most efficient short-term strategy for increasing revenue is to reduce expenses.

Within this context, consider a situation where several directors decide to increase the control mechanisms at all levels of the company in order to achieve their financial objectives. They hire analysts to develop sophisticated tools for measuring the employees' performance and the management of operations to the smallest detail. The directors find themselves with a multitude of analyses or dashboards, much like those in a cockpit. The greatest challenge with this strategy lies in interpreting the results. What are they going to do with all these indicators? Who will interpret them? How will they be interpreted? Will the employees be consulted about validating the methodology? How will the employees be affected?

All too often, control mechanisms are developed and analyzed without the knowledge and input of the employees, and when the reports are published, they progressively become the company's new standard for the objectives to be attained. This strategy has many advantages for streamlining the business, but if not implemented well, there can be several traps.

The mechanisms used to control the budget and the employees' productivity are important, but they must not become the company's sole focus. This is one of the challenges that several team leaders face. Here is an example of what frequently happens when the control mechanisms become the directors' number one focus: An ambitious manager who wants to look good to his superiors will encourage his employees to prioritize the tasks related specifically to the report parameters. What happens next? This attitude of managing to parameters will have a negative impact on job quality, customer service, and teamwork, because employees will focus on the result itself more than on the process of achieving the result. It is also likely that employees will feel that the organization no longer trusts their business acumen and intuition. Resilient employees will lose their motivation, since there is no longer any place for personal initiatives, innovative practices, and "common sense" at work.

This approach of managing the business by only considering the numbers has harmful impacts on the work environment. It will make the employees view themselves as having a low value and, as a consequence, they will do the strict minimum required to earn their salaries. The employees will develop an attitude of disengagement at work as discussed in the previous chapter.

The other trap concerns the lack of communication and the application of these control mechanisms with respect to the employees. Transparency in the communications between management and the employees is the most important element for a successful reorganization. We received several testimonials on this topic.

A nurse working in a hospital shared that, as a result of the most recent reorganization, her boss is now in charge of several departments. She doesn't see her anymore and is no longer able to speak with her. She feels like a cog in a large system, and the work environment is no longer motivating. In addition, the control mechanisms put in place limit her initiative with respect to how she performs her tasks and the time required to complete them. Her work gets done and she obeys the directives, but nothing more. She doesn't even react to aberrations anymore, since she could be perceived as having a negative attitude. Resignedly, she observed: "Our leaders are now technocrats who do nothing but look at columns of figures."

It is not only the employees who are affected by this type of management which prioritizes control mechanisms. Team leaders are also impacted, one of them informing that following a reorganization, the new flavor of the month is to increase that the mechanisms for controlling work done by the representatives. The company's executives have developed a tool for measuring all of the performance indicators for his team, the budgets and the resources. He agrees with the principles of this new tool; however, he is concerned by the fact that the senior managers only interpret the figures without considering the reality of the work environment in the field. He and his colleagues have reached the point where they focus solely on the dashboard, so as to look good. Disappointed, he told me: "They want figures for their sausage machine? Well, they'll get them! By trying to control everything, they've eliminated leadership and initiative. We work for the machine, not the clients."

Paul, an employee a few years from retirement in a large company, confirms a dehumanizing process:

> *Following numerous reorganizations, we're now managed by technocrats who are afraid to take the initiative and only keep their eyes focused on their figures. There is no longer any collaboration among my colleagues. Everyone is on edge and afraid of losing their job. That's sad because I could become a mentor for the young employees and give them the benefits of my experience and my expertise, but that has no value within the company. I've given up and I do my job, but nothing more. There are so many changes and so many contradictions in the priorities that I longer know which way is up.*

We recognize that performance indicators and control mechanisms are usually well-accepted by employees and team leaders. What hurts people deeply and causes them to lose their motivation is the incorrect interpretation of the figures and the implementation of new processes that disregard the employees' reality. When an obsession with norms means that budget considerations take precedence over the client and the quality of the work done by the employees, the *raison d'être* of the company or public service organization is lost.

Allison, a manager in a health service organization, described a situation that occurred in a residence for the elderly:

> *Senior management sent a strategic guideline to all managers encouraging them, but not requiring them, to eliminate overtime worked by the employees. An unexpected situation occurred: a few patients came down with a viral gastroenteritis. The housekeeping employee was overwhelmed with work and could no longer perform his tasks to clean and disinfect the facility adequately. What did the technocrat manager do? He decided to apply the guideline to the letter and did not authorize overtime. As a result of that decision, the virus spread quickly within the facility and caused a serious epidemic that had harmful effects on the health of the patients and the operations of the residence, which was unable to take in any new patients.*

This is just one example of a penny-pinching control mechanism instituted by a technocrat who gives priority to the results of his quarterly report to the detriment of his role within the organization—namely the health of the patients. All in all, these savings resulted in additional costs for other departments, including the nursing department, which had to manage an epidemic. This is a good example of "silo" management, in which people base decisions on the tree standing in front of them while ignoring the impact on the entire forest. With respect to managing a team, there are situations in which common sense must take precedence over the nitpicking application of procedures and control mechanisms. In order to respond to a specific need, a true leader will have the courage to make a decision that will go against the guideline suggested by his superiors, and he will be able to justify doing so to them. This type of leadership will be noticed by his employees and will ensure that they remain motivated, dedicated to their work, and prepared to do more when an unexpected situation occurs.

In order to implement a successful reorganization, the company needs leaders at all hierarchical levels, including first line managers who work directly with the employees. A climate of mutual trust must be established in order to change the employees' behaviors and habits. Control measures are necessary, but they must not become the company's *modus operandi*, since that will eliminate any chance that the company's new strategy will succeed. The employees will feel stressed out, will lose confidence in themselves and the organization, and will no longer be productive. They will no longer inform the directors about new, creative ideas or obstacles. In such a work environment, the right hand will not know what the left is doing.

What is the profile sought for a team leader following a reorganization?

In the case of a reorganization involving job cuts, legal considerations, work standards, seniority, and past performance often take precedence in the selection of managers. Be that as it may, the team leaders selected will have a thankless and difficult role to play in the weeks following the reorganization. They will have to earn the trust of all of their employees and build a performing and healthy work environment in order to attain corporate objectives. Research has clearly demonstrated that it is the immediate superior who makes all the difference in employee commitment when it comes to creating a positive and performing work environment.

Managers with a technocrat personality and limited emotional intelligence skills should not be placed in positions that require the direct supervision of employees following a reorganization. These technocrats are useful for the company, but should be assigned a role to provide technical support for the directors and not as team leaders supervising a group of employees.

An employee told coauthor Nicole Labbe that, following the reorganization, a simple stroll through the offices was revealing. There was one department filled with joy, while another looked like a funeral parlor. Yet, both departments had been affected in a similar manner with job cuts and reorganizations of the employees' responsibilities. What was the reason for this difference? The team leader's leadership style was responsible to a large degree.

What is the profile of a good team leader in the context of a reorganization? Which skills should be considered a priority when selecting a team leader? In addition to the technical and strategic skills specific to each organization, these leaders should have competencies that are all too often ignored or not considered priorities in the selection of team leaders: emotional intelligence and effective collaboration.

In addition to emotional intelligence and effective collaboration, the leader should also have excellent communication skills. These qualities will enable the team leader to understand and highlight the strengths of each employee. He must have courage to deal with difficult situations involving both superiors and employees. This leader must also be a team player who collaborates actively with the entire organization beyond his own department. A good understanding of the political issues within the organization will help the leader develop solid business relationships with colleagues.

Several studies have been published on emotional intelligence and the skills for effective collaboration. In the following pages, we will provide an overview of various practical applications of these concepts.

Emotional intelligence

Today, no one could imagine working without a smartphone, a computer, access to video conferences, and other electronic devices and applications to improve their efficiency. However, an electronic device can never replace the power of emotional intelligence when it comes to interacting with colleagues and clients.

We do not intend to make an exhaustive analysis of emotional intelligence. Experts have already published a wide variety of relevant books on the topic. Our goal is to highlight examples of behaviors or attitudes that could provide food for thought. We should all have an interest in better understanding the skills involved in emotional intelligence, regardless of our position in the hierarchy at work. Improving one's emotional intelligence is a daily challenge, since situations that require such skills occur several times per day. During the implementation of organizational changes, several employees will be on edge and will find it difficult to control their emotions. It is specifically in situations of acute stress that people with great emotional intelligence skills will become authentic, inspiring, and courageous leaders. Capable of demonstrating their humanity, they will be appreciated and respected.

The term "emotional intelligence" means much more than charisma and sociability. An extroverted person will not necessarily have greater emotional intelligence. At the same time, a person who is naturally introverted may have great skills in emotional intelligence.

First, what is the definition of emotional intelligence? "Emotional intelligence is your ability to recognize and understand emotions in yourself and others, and your ability to use this awareness to manage your behavior and relationships. Emotional intelligence is the 'something' in each of us that is a bit intangible. It affects how we manage, behave, or navigate social complexities, and make personal decisions that achieve positive results."[30]

In today's work world, the success of a leader is closely linked to his interpersonal skills for perceiving and understanding his emotions and those of others in order to use them adequately to solve the problems faced on a daily basis.

Researchers have identified several skills that characterize emotional intelligence. Some of them are: recognizing one's emotions, self-affirmation, authenticity, self-control, adaptability, resilience, recognition of others' emotions, empathy, collaboration, and conflict management. They have classified these skills in two categories:

1. Personal competencies: self-awareness and self-management
2. Social competencies: social awareness and relationship management

Evaluating these skills and the extent to which they are applied consciously or unconsciously at work, is justified in the assessment of emotional intelligence competencies.

Instead of using the traditional approach to list behaviors that demonstrate exemplary emotional intelligence, we have opted for a different approach. Dr. Travis Bradberry, coauthor of the best seller *Emotional Intelligence 2.0*,[31] conducted research on close to one million people, studying the behaviors related to emotional intelligence. His survey demonstrated that 90% of the people who perform best at work, the "Top Performers," have a very high degree of emotional intelligence.

---

30. Travis Bradberry, Jean Greaves, Patrick M. Lencioni, *Emotional Intelligence 2.0*, (San Diego: TalentSmart, 2009) 17.
31. Ibid.

He also conducted research to identify the behaviors that demonstrate a low degree of emotional intelligence.[32] Here is a brief overview of his list of signs demonstrating a low level of emotional intelligence and how to overcome them. Our goal is to suggest an opportunity to do some introspective thinking about the situations that drive many of us to adopt these behaviors. The beauty of emotional intelligence is that it is a dynamic concept that makes improvement possible each day.

"You get stressed out easily."[33] Ignoring your emotions causes them to build up and transform into stress and anxiety. Your emotional intelligence (EQ) skills will help you manage this stress by enabling you to identify the specific emotions resulting from a stressful situation so as to understand them better and take action to manage them differently.

"You have difficulty asserting yourself."[34] Saying "no" is difficult for many people. Research has demonstrated that people who find it hard to say no face a greater risk of being stressed out. Self-aware people with emotional intelligence avoid phrases such as "I don't think I can … " or "I'm not sure that …" They do not hesitate to assert themselves and say "no" from time to time, tactfully and diplomatically.

"You have a limited emotional vocabulary."[35] "All people experience emotions, but only 36% can accurately identify them as they

---

32. Travis Bradberry, "11 Signs That You Lack Emotional Intelligence," TalentSmart, 2019, www.talentsmart.com.
33. Ibid.
34. Ibid.
35. Ibid.

occur.[36] Finding it difficult to identify emotions can result in a lack of understanding and lead to decisions that are irrational, made out of context, and counterproductive. People with acute emotional intelligence master their emotions because they understand them and use a broad vocabulary to describe them accurately.

"You make assumptions quickly and defend them vehemently."[37] Stubbornly defending your own opinion while ignoring those of others can cause conflicts and lead to poor decisions. "Emotionally intelligent people let their thoughts marinate because they know that initial reactions are driven by emotions."[38] This approach allows them to develop their opinion while considering the other options possible. "Then, they communicate their developed idea in the most effective way possible, taking into account the needs and opinions of their audience."[39]

"You hold grudges."[40] The negative emotions that come from the past can cause useless stress. When you are faced with a threat, the body's survival mechanisms are activated, creating the strengths needed to face the enemy. Is this reaction necessary when the threat is ancient history? This additional stress can have devastating consequences on your physical and mental health. Emotional intelligence skills help people to know how to avoid stress and the harm caused by holding grudges. Forgiving someone not only makes you feel better, but can contribute to good physical and mental health.

---

36. Ibid.
37. Ibid.
38. Ibid.
39. Ibid.
40. Ibid.

"You don't let go of mistakes."[41] Constantly going back over your mistakes causes anxiety and increases the chances you will make the same mistakes again. It is preferable to keep your mistakes at a safe distance; however, without ignoring them. In fact, any failure is a learning opportunity that will help you react better and adapt to future situations. In this case, it is important to forgive yourself and use your own errors for personal growth. Recalling your mistakes without dwelling on them is a subtle balancing act that requires good self-awareness.

"You often feel misunderstood."[42] People feel misunderstood when they don't deliver their message in a way that others understand. Communicating ideas is a constant challenge, even for people with good emotional intelligence skills. These people use their skills to decode the reactions of others and adjust their message so as to make sure it is interpreted correctly.

"You don't know your triggers."[43] Knowing yourself is the key to responding adequately to any offense. Emotional intelligence skills help people to become confident and open-minded. They have no difficulty laughing at themselves or accepting jokes from others, because they easily understand the difference between humor and insult.

"You don't get angry."[44] Emotional intelligence does not mean that you are always nice and never get angry. Instead, it is the art of managing your emotions and understanding those of others in

---

41. Ibid.
42. Ibid.
43. Ibid.
44. Ibid.

order to achieve the best possible outcomes. Emotionally intelligent people use their negative and positive emotions in appropriate situations.

"You blame other people for how they make you feel."[45] It is important to take responsibility for your own emotions. You have 100% control over your feelings. Your response and reaction to any situation is ultimately your decision and you choose how you are going to feel.

"You're easily offended."[46] This is often where we distort reality. Emotionally intelligent people are able to draw the line between humor and offense. They will ask for clarification before jumping to conclusions regarding another person's actions or remarks.

These questions represent a brief overview of the self-awareness needed to assess your degree of emotional intelligence. Living through a reorganization is a challenge at all levels. You find yourself in the middle of a storm, experiencing intense emotions that can be positive or negative. And our colleagues are in the same boat, traveling through the same storm. In this context, emotional intelligence skills can be required at any time. How can you get your bearings and head out of the storm? First, you have to identify and recognize your emotions, which involves being aware of and knowing yourself. Then, you have to learn to control them and manage them adequately. This requires adaptability and resilience. Healthy self-management is the prerequisite for interacting with work colleagues. Next, you will need empathy for recognizing and understanding the emotions of others. Listening to others while

---

45. Ibid.
46. Ibid.

controlling your own emotions will facilitate cooperation and the resolution of conflicts with work colleagues. It's easy to say, but sometimes hard to do.

A reorganization is an opportunity to improve your emotional intelligence skills. Here are a few tips:

- ✓ know your strong points and your weaknesses
- ✓ be curious about others and listen to them
- ✓ give without expecting something in return
- ✓ put yourself in the shoes of your boss or your colleague
- ✓ don't let yourself be overwhelmed by the anger of toxic people
- ✓ don't strive for perfection
- ✓ look for small wins and celebrate them
- ✓ don't let anyone ruin your happiness
- ✓ don't forget that we only have one chance at today, and that tomorrow is another day

Remember that you feel the way you choose to feel. Your reactions and responses are 100% within your control.

Becoming an effective collaborator

Effective collaboration becomes an increasingly important issue in today's changing workplace. Organizational changes often involve the abolition of a department or the merger between two or more departments. With the globalization of activities, work teams are divided between several regions or countries. The organization's success depends on the interconnectivity of the departments, the teamwork of the units located here and there throughout the world, and the elimination of silos. Effective collaboration is a strategic objective of the business plan of most companies, but it is a challenge to implement in a post-reorganization environment where new administrative structures are created. The survivors must quickly learn how to work as a team and collaborate with their colleagues, some of whom have arrived recently from another department or region. Keep in mind that these survivors may also be managers who are not happy in their new roles. Achieving effective collaboration from all employees is a significant challenge in this post-reorganization environment, especially since survivor-related behaviors run counterintuitively to it.

In the previous chapter, we noted that it is frequent for a survivor to feel isolated, to be unwilling to share information, to feel unappreciated, to not trust the directors fully, and so on. This type of behavior is normal and frequent in the case of survivors. Each employee has their own reasons for acting in this manner. In order to look good and demonstrate a positive attitude, the employee may loudly declare that collaboration is important. But, in actual fact, he only shares required information and nothing more. In the experience of coauthor Nicole Labbe, these behaviors are frequent and even continue for several years following a painful reorganization.

The politically correct concept of collaboration is on the lips of all in post-reorganization language. Unfortunately, this collaboration is passive in many cases, since each employee remains on guard, seeking to save their job, avoiding additional work, and preserving their expertise as examples. It is difficult to collaborate openly when you don't trust your colleagues. On the other hand, there are employees who will cooperate with everyone in order to compensate for the others, and they will find themselves with an additional workload that is difficult to manage.

The team leader has an important role to play in identifying the behaviors related to survivor syndrome and taking action with those concerned in order to re-establish the bond of trust. He must also demonstrate an extraordinary capacity for collaboration so as to facilitate synergy with other departments and also encourage his employees to collaborate effectively to form a solid team. How to become successful?

In order to understand the impact of the team leader's capacity for creating a collaborative environment, let us clarify a few self-evident facts obtained from research into the topic.

The definition of collaboration refers to an action that is conducted efficiently *with* a person or a group in order to attain a *common goal*. It is specifically this common goal that determines the degree to which an employee agrees to collaborate.

In an article entitled "Collaborative Overload," published in the January 2016 issue of the *Harvard Business Review*,[47] authors Rob Cross, Reb Rebele, and Adam Grant studied close to three hundred companies to evaluate the efficiency of collaboration at work. They observed that the amount of time dedicated to teamwork, meetings, and collaborative activities has increased more than 50% over the past twenty years. Moreover, they also noted that 20% to 35% of effective collaboration came from a limited group of 3% to 5% of the employees. When they asked the directors to identify these employees from a list, most of the bosses did not know these performing collaborators. Surprising?

The concept of collaboration is venerated in all organizations, but we must ask ourselves just how efficient it is. An excess of collaboration that generates useless additional work can lead to

---

47. Rob Cross, Reb Rebele, and Adam Grant, "Collaborative Overload," *Harvard Business Review*, Vol. 94, no. 1/2 (January-February 2016), 74–79.

burnout and inefficiency. A lack of collaboration encourages a culture of silo management. Are the employees who collaborate sufficiently recognized and valued for their contributions? How can they be, if their employers don't even know who they are? These questions spark reflection on how to implement an effective culture of collaboration.

As a first step, we need to establish benchmarks for clarifying exactly what efficient collaboration is. The initial objective is to encourage individual leadership so as to improve the company's efficiency, both within and among departments. Efficient collaboration is the art of using a colleague's expertise to improve, accelerate, or clarify a project or a procedure.

Above all, it does not mean attending all of the meetings held by other departments without having specific objectives. It also does not involve cc'ing all colleagues in an email. Do you have the impression that you are wasting your time attending a meeting? Receiving pointless emails? This will be an opportunity for you to consider the measures to be taken to improve the efficiency of the collaboration within your work group.

In this context, the team leader plays a crucial role in establishing the benchmarks for efficient collaboration within his team. Moreover, he must make sure that he maintains a balance between recognizing individual accomplishments as compared to efficient collaboration. Here are a few suggestions for promoting efficient collaboration:

- ✓ preach by example and share best practices
- ✓ evaluate the supply and demand for collaborative activities and the time required to complete them for each employee
- ✓ redistribute the responsibilities as needed to prevent burnout

- ✓ recognize and reward the employees who collaborate efficiently
- ✓ clarify the common goal of a collaborative project to ensure that it is realistic and significant for all of the employees involved
- ✓ make sure that all discussions take place in a climate of trust and mutual respect; no disrespect should be tolerated
- ✓ accept the fact that errors are made and use them as learning opportunities
- ✓ highlight the strengths of each member of the team and trust them
- ✓ decentralize the decision-making process so that the employees feel empowered and to encourage buy-in
- ✓ celebrate small successes

In his article *"How to become a champion collaborator,"* Mark Lipkin describes the secret formula for champion collaborators: *"Champion collaborators help others succeed in a way that motivates others to invest more time and resources with them."*[48]

We are all convinced of the importance of efficient collaboration. The next step is: How to build a performing team, taking the different personalities of our employees into consideration? There are always colleagues with whom it is easier to collaborate and others with whom it is more difficult. The team leader is responsible for knowing his employees' personality types and determining what makes each employee tick. Here are some examples of questions to ask in order to deepen your understanding of an employee's profile in their work environment.

---

48. Mike Lipkin, *"How to Become a Champion Collaborator,"* (2019) http://www.mikelipkin.com/how-to-become-a-champion-collaborator/.

- ✓ What sets the employee into action?
- ✓ How does the employee approach his work? Methodically? Intuitively?
- ✓ How does the employee behave in a team meeting?
- ✓ What frustrates the employee the most?
- ✓ What is the best approach for communicating with each employee?
- ✓ How can collaboration be improved?

Researchers for the firm Deloitte made an exhaustive study of close to 190,000 individuals in order to better understand the various personality types in the workplace. The results are impressive. This study was published in the March 2017 issue of the *Harvard Business Review*.[49] The study identified four types of employees:

1. **Pioneers**: Extroverted, spontaneous, creative, give priority to major guidelines, no attention to detail. Don't like rules or processes. Bring energy and imagination to the team.
2. **Drivers**: Logical, quantitative, competitive, curious, like to solve problems. Don't like indecisiveness and inefficiency. Stimulated by challenges.
3. **Integrators**: Diplomatic, empathetic, traditional, collaborator, respectful, focused on relationships. Don't like conflicts. Bring a sense of cohesion to the team, value collaboration.

---

49. Suzanne M. Johnson-Vickberg and Kim Christfort, "Pioneers, Drivers, Integrators, and Guardians," *Harvard Business Review*, Vol. 95, No. 2, (March–April 2017), 52.

4. **Guardians**: Methodical, reserved, focused on details, practical, structured, loyal. Don't like ambiguity and a lack of order. Bring stability and rigor to the team.

A performing team needs employees of all four personality types. The role of the team leader is to make the best use of the strengths of each employee and to encourage the different personalities to work together in mutual respect and with a common goal. The guardian and pioneer personalities are the complete opposites. Same for the driver and the integrator personalities. It is a huge challenge to work closely with a colleague whose personality is diametrically opposed to one's own, but doing so will enable the team to improve and perform better. During a team meeting, the pioneers and drivers will take up a lot of space to the detriment of the integrators and guardians. It should not be taken for granted that those who remain silent during a meeting do not have opinions about the topic discussed. Certain employees feel more comfortable sharing their opinions in a face-to-face setting, or in small groups. The same principle applies to the management of a project in which the role of guardians is critical, because they are the ones who will integrate all of the details in order to complete the task successfully.

The team leader plays a key role in actively involving each employee, based on their personality and the way they work. His role can be compared to the conductor of an orchestra who knows how to integrate each musician in order to obtain a flawless performance.

The skill profile required of a team leader following a reorganization has evolved a great deal in recent years, as a result of new technologies and corporate cultures that are focused on change. The ability to develop emotional intelligence and skill at collaborating efficiently is now essential for success. Building a performing team while making the most of the personality type of each employee is the key to success for standing out from the competition. So now, how can you plan Day 1 with the new team?

Day 1 following a reorganization

The day following the reorganization, you are appointed the team leader within the company's new structure. You are now responsible for a team of twelve. You have never worked closely with six of these individuals. Everyone is a survivor, including yourself. You must make up for the decline in sales that led to the reorganization. Management has high expectations for your leadership and your ability to communicate the company's new vision quickly. What should you do, and not do, on Day 1?

1. Meeting with each survivor

The first meeting with each survivor can be stressful for the team leader, because he doesn't know how the new employee will react. This is a stimulating challenge for emotional intelligence skills! Consider starting the conversation with a new employee by asking him to speak about himself, his family, and his personal interests. What motivates him at work, and what gives him personal satisfaction? The employee may feel a need to discuss the reorganization and ask questions about the people who left, and may make judgments about some survivors. Under these circumstances, it is important to avoid making any judgment about the decisions that were made.

A conversation with each individual must take place on Day 1. And then, an individual face-to-face meeting with each employee should take place within two weeks after the reorganization. All of these conversations are important for developing trust and discussing mutual expectations, which are the key components of the employee-team leader relationship. Another face-to-face meeting should be planned in the weeks following the reorganization to agree on the terms of the psychological contract that we will discuss in the next chapter.

Rachel, an experienced manager, summed up the task:

> *I compare Day 1 to the first thirty seconds for making a good impression during a meeting with someone you don't know. These first moments are critical, since they will be engraved in the mind of each of my employees. This is the time when active listening and emotional intelligence are the most needed.*
>
> *The number one priority is to organize a face-to-face meeting with each employee within the next few days. The place of the meeting is important for facilitating the discussion. I prefer a coffee shop or a quiet bistro outside the workplace. I prepare each meeting carefully based on what I know of the employee's fragility and their potential reaction following the reorganization. In fact, I make sure I turn my cell phone off and I clear my mind of all frustrations so that I can listen to my employee 100%. I insist on demonstrating active*

listening, empathy, sincerity, realism, and authenticity so as to develop a relationship based on mutual trust. In any reorganization, there is a loss of trust in management. It's necessary to give the employee a chance to express their emotions, fears, and expectations so as to alleviate the negative impacts of the reorganization on the employee's personal situation. I want to encourage an attitude of resilience in order to prevent any risk of dropping out and disengagement. Moreover, I want to obtain each employee's commitment to me as their team leader and to the new structure, the new team, and the corporate vision.

Once, an employee who was dissatisfied with his new position refused to join my team. I reacted by asking him to attend the first team meeting before making his final decision. The day after the meeting, he informed me that he was pleased to join my team because he had felt heard, accepted, and valued.

2. Organizing the first team meeting

Once again, timing is crucial. This meeting should be organized as quickly as possible, in the days after the new team is established. There are three fundamental objectives for this meeting:

1. To learn about all of the team members and to develop each individual's self-esteem by asking them to speak

about their career and how they can contribute to the team's success
2. To discuss the new vision of the company, department, and objectives
3. To agree on the basic rules for the manner in which the team will function, including ground rules about respecting others and efficient collaboration

The success of the meeting depends on the flexibility and emotional intelligence the team leader will be able to demonstrate so as to ensure that each member of the team feels listened to and respected. Once, coauthor Nicole Labbe took two hours to let all of the team members introduce themselves. In the following days and weeks, the experienced employees told her that these two hours had served as a spark plug, motivating them with their work because they all felt listened to and valued. Ideally, this meeting should be face-to-face and conference calls should be avoided. If travel is impossible, videoconferencing is most appropriate, since all of the participants can be seen in person and it is possible to ensure that they are all in active listening mode during the discussions. Make sure that cell phones are turned off and stored out of reach! You don't want any distractions.

3. Identifying potential traps and how to avoid them

The team leader must implement the changes required by upper management as quickly as possible, while listening to the employees affected by those changes. It is a fine balancing act in an environment where the unexpected, the stress, and the urgency to act can potentially have negative consequences on the team. Several traps that occur frequently the first few months following a reorganization include: mismanagement of communications, additional work, the fear of speaking out, and the lack of collaboration. We will discuss these pitfalls briefly and suggest possible solutions.

Managing communications. In a post-reorganization situation, there is an abundance of communications, some of which are transmitted in an emergency context to deal with unforeseen adjustments. Sometimes an email written in inappropriate or error-prone language can create a tsunami of negative reactions and demotivate employees. It is important to consider the increased sensitivity of the employees with respect to the slightest hitch in communications. The basic rule is mutual respect, transparency, sincerity, and credibility in all written and oral communications. Before pressing send, pause and ask yourself if the message fulfils the THINK principle: is it thoughtful, helpful, inspiring, necessary, and kind?

Managing the additional work, newness and unpredictable situations. There is always additional work in a post-reorganization context. The need to adapt to changes and unforeseeable situations contribute to this additional work. An employee in a new position may quickly feel overwhelmed. In order to survive, we must establish priorities. Instead of working on ten projects without being able to see the light at the end of the tunnel, it is preferable to make sure that one or two projects are completed quickly and well in order to reduce pressure and celebrate a small victory. We should not forget that the additional efforts made by the employees must be acknowledged and rewarded. Why not give an employee a few hours off from time to time?

Managing the fear of speaking up. Employees often hesitate to speak up and ask questions about an ambiguous situation, or to denounce unacceptable behavior. We have noticed that, even several years after a reorganization, employees are still afraid to speak up. This is a good example of how embedded survivor syndrome can become. The team leader must develop a relationship of trust with his employees and, above all, encourage freedom of expression in a constructive context.

Developing team spirit and efficient collaboration. The key to developing team spirit is having confidence in yourself and trust in others. This mutual confidence will result in a win-win collaborative environment that will enable the team to achieve its objectives. In any team, there are natural leaders and those who prefer to adopt a more discrete attitude. A talented team leader is able to quickly identify the personality type and work style of each employee so as to highlight their strengths and develop synergy. The team leader must listen and also establish clear objectives concerning the expectations and attitudes required.

As a result of today's environment, in which each individual works in front of a computer often wearing earphones, many employees feel alone and isolated at work. Some can work an entire day without speaking to a single work colleague. It is difficult to develop team spirit and encourage collaboration in such a context. The team leader is responsible for encouraging the development of social relationships and collaboration among his employees. Additionally, research to support this point has demonstrated that the employees who develop solid relationships with their work colleagues are more committed to their work, perform better, and have a lower rate of absenteeism.[50]

The challenge for the team leader is that he must work to improve the company's performance and rebuild the team quickly, with limited or non-existent resources.

This list of traps illustrates the scope of the challenge to be faced in a post-reorganization environment. Keep in mind that the team leader is a human being with strengths and weaknesses and, in several cases, is also a survivor who has experienced uncertainty about losing his position, just like his employees.

Succeeding as a team leader

We don't claim to have all the answers to being a successful team leader, since each company has a unique work environment that contributes to success. However, we want to share some tips based on testimonials, literature on the topic, and our own personal experience. Here are some of the elements that can help a team leader perform better:

- ✓ take care of yourself
- ✓ communication should be frequent, transparent, honest and authentic (use the THINK principle); any ambiguity should be clarified, since it can quickly cause employees to lose their motivation

---

50. McKEE, Anne, "Happiness Traps: How we Sabotage Ourselves at Work," *Harvard Business Review*, Vol. 95, No. 5, September–October 2017, 66.

- ✓ identify a limited number of team priorities (ideally no more than three) with a specific timetable; refer to this timetable under all circumstances
- ✓ set the example and demonstrate emotional intelligence at all times
- ✓ get to know each employee quickly and find out what motivates them and what they are interested in
- ✓ identify the employees who demonstrate positive leadership within their team and use them as ambassadors of the changes that need to be made
- ✓ make yourself available to discuss the challenges to be overcome in a transparent manner; act as a coach, and even as a consultant, to help and encourage employees
- ✓ help your employees recognize the behaviors of survivor syndrome and act quickly to overcome them effectively (common examples: working in silos, risk aversion, disengagement, negative attitude, fear of making mistakes, etc.)
- ✓ manage the employees' stress proactively; take small steps at a time and keep in mind the following principle, which is supported by neuroscience research: *"What's the only way to raise employee performance at a time of stress? By reducing stress!"*[51]
- ✓ have frequent and individual discussions with each employee to clarify their role and responsibilities; discuss mutual expectations concerning the position, personal development, and career progress; establish clear and realistic objectives and priorities with the employees concerned; use

---

51. Sonia Lupien, *Well Stressed: Manage Stress Before it Turns Toxic*, HarperCollins e-books, Toronto, 2012, 55.

coaching techniques to improve knowledge and correct shortcomings[52]
- ✓ create a work environment in which each employee feels confident to offer his unique best and is appreciated; acknowledge the leadership and accountability of each employee; provide information about progress, developments, and accomplishments; encourage efficient collaboration and celebrate each small victory
- ✓ be the best advocate for your team
- ✓ encourage your employees, give them feedback quickly about a good initiative or even a mistake; show them that you trust them completely and that their initiatives are welcome; ask them for their opinions and acknowledge their contributions
- ✓ don't tolerate the unacceptable; an employee with a negative attitude or performance that does not satisfy expectations must be dealt with quickly
- ✓ above all, don't forget to enjoy yourself; have fun while working and transmit this enthusiasm.

---

52. Ferdinand Fournies, *Coaching for Improved Work Performance*, McGraw-Hill, New York, 2000.

TO SUMMARIZE

In this chapter, we have discussed the challenges faced by the team leader in a post-reorganization context. His hierarchical position as an intermediary between the executive directors and the employees is similar to that of a tightrope walker trying to keep his balance when facing gusts of wind. This wind comes from both the leadership and the employees. The executive team wants to turn the page quickly on the reorganization and achieve their financial and corporate objectives. Several will tend to increase the mechanisms for controlling the employees' performance and apply pressure on them to increase their productivity. A popular expression is "to do more with less." The wind also comes from the employees, who find themselves in a very demanding work environment that is filled with uncertainties as a result of the adjustments required following the reorganization. The additional workload is also a challenge for all survivors.

Our acrobatic team leader will have to demonstrate great capacity for emotional intelligence in order to earn his employees' trust. He is responsible for developing a work climate that is based on respect and trust for his employees. In order to feel happy and perform well, the employees must feel they have the approval of their boss. They must also trust their boss and feel able to discuss difficult situations with him. The channels of communication must be open on both sides. During a reorganization, the enemy to be defeated is ambiguity—which is not always easy.

In short, a well-prepared team leader has the opportunity to build a performing and dynamic team once again; however, the challenges are greater to achieving this in a post-reorganization environment. If the leader acts quickly and deliberately, employing his emotional intelligence and collaboration skills, the team will once again be on the path of success.

Chapter 4

WORKING ON MY DEVELOPMENT

Working in a constantly changing environment is both psychologically and emotionally challenging. Being transferred to another position or finding yourself with new responsibilities is demanding. In most cases, the organization has high expectations and tight timelines where employees are required to perform rapidly in their new assignment. With limited resources for staff training, employees are often called upon to train themselves and learn on the job. This situation puts additional stress on everyone's shoulders that can lead to a sense of loss of control with negative effects on self-confidence.

Our discussions with many employees and managers have shown us that the people who best adapt to multiple changes at work and the uncertainty of losing their jobs are the resilient ones who invest the most on their own development to acquire diversified skills and competencies. Being diversified helps them to feel more confident in the face of losing their job because their broader skill set enables a Plan B, C, or D.

This chapter is intended to provide practical solutions and strategies to work on your development. First, we will discuss the mutual employee-employer psychological contract. Then, we will provide strategies to take control of your career development. The third section will address the challenges of working in an atmosphere that has become toxic. Finally, you will be able to pick and choose ideas for surviving from the survivor's tool box.

Discussing the psychological contract with my boss

An employee who joins a new organization generally has a positive opinion of their manager and the company's vision. This employee trusts the organizational leaders, is dedicated to their work, and has a positive and creative attitude. On the other hand, this employee was hired because he satisfies the profile needed for getting the job done. The employer-employee relationship needs two essential components to ensure organizational success: two-way trust and employee commitment.

A reorganization involving several job cuts has a direct impact on the trust the employees have in the management team and the employees' level of commitment. Not all employees react in the same manner. Some maintain a positive and committed attitude, while others develop a negative attitude. Why? Because an employee's behavior is the result of each individual's perceptions of their work and their level of engagement to accomplish it. This is referred to as the psychological contract between the employee and the employer.

There are two types of contracts that bind the employer and the employee: the formal employment contract and the psychological one. The formal contract defines reciprocal obligations such as remuneration, work hours, and other aspects of a legal or ethical nature. The psychological contract defines the tacit relationships, mutual expectations, and unwritten agreements between the employer and the employee. It represents the notion of trust in the employer-employee relationship.

This contract is implicit and intangible, and concerns the mutual expectations of each party. The psychological contract defines what the employer expects from the employee and what the employee expects from the employer. There are a few topics to be discussed by an employee and his immediate superior, such as: respective expectations, teleworking, flexible hours, recognition of efforts and accomplishments, career path, contribution to corporate culture, autonomy for making decisions, empowerment, form and type of mutual communication, development of new skills, performance appraisal, etc. In most cases, these topics will be discussed verbally, in keeping with the corporate culture and the management style of the employee's immediate superior. Individual perceptions are part of many aspects of the psychological contract. Is my superior satisfied with the effort I made to facilitate the implementation of a new system? Should I cc my superior in all of the emails I send? If the employee feels that his employer is not fulfilling all of the commitments contained in the mutual expectations, the trust relationship may be damaged. The same may happen in the case of an employer who is dissatisfied with an employee's performance or attitude at work.

The psychological contract between the employer and the employee is put to the test following a reorganization that involves job cuts. The tacit agreement concerning employment security and career progression is challenged. Can I still trust my employer? What about the promotion he promised me in six months?

Since today's work environment is constantly changing, employees must change their perceptions with respect to the jobs they hold. The time when it was possible to find a "job for life" is a thing of the past for a lot of employees. The former psychological contract under which the employer adopted a paternalistic attitude toward its employees has been abandoned. The employee can no longer depend solely on their employer for job security and help in guiding and developing his career.

Taking control of my career development

Reorganizations and job cuts have served to redefine the employer-employee relationship. It is now a business relationship. The employer seeks to increase its profits by capitalizing on a team of dynamic employees who will help it attain its short- and medium-term goals. But, if the business environment deteriorates, expenses and jobs will be re-evaluated and possibly cut. Promising long-term employment to an employee is impossible, regardless of their performance. The budgets for employee training and development are either reduced or nonexistent. Employment security is utopic for employees in the private sector as well as for an increasing number of employees in the public sector. The work relationship between the employer and the employee is more and more self-centered. Today's employee is a service provider who negotiates a work contract with a company. The duration of the contract is not specified, and the two parties can terminate it at any time.

Job security is a thing of the past. To reinforce this, today each employee or manager is responsible for their own personal development and career progression. They must optimize their own "market value," taking the initiative to improve their skills and their capacity to become a service supplier that is attractive to future employers. Marketability becomes an essential bargaining argument for obtaining a promotion or a position with different or more responsibilities. This principle applies to both the employee who wants to remain with the company and one who is considering a new position. Every employee has a market value and needs to make the most of opportunities to increase their employability, regardless of their position or hierarchical level.

Here's a small test for you. Look at yourself and answer the following questions:

- ✓ Am I unable to picture myself working anywhere but for this organization?
- ✓ Do I feel that I would be worthless if I were to lose my job tomorrow?
- ✓ Do I rely solely on my employer to manage my personal development and my career progression?
- ✓ Did I experience a feeling of betrayal following the reorganization?
- ✓ Do I believe that my employer will take care of me until I retire?
- ✓ Am I deeply afraid of losing my job?

If you answered yes to one of these questions, we suggest that you re-evaluate your relationship with your employer and the degree to which you depend on your job in order to avoid any future disappointment.

And now, how do you take control of your career development and discuss the psychological contract with your employer? The first step involves considering your perception of your job and your expectations concerning your employer. You have to dismantle your dependence on your position. An employment contract is not a marriage for life. Regardless of their position in the company, each employee must adopt an entrepreneurial attitude toward their employer and manage their own career, taking the initiative in terms of their skill development to improve their market value. Since reorganizations often entail an increased workload, the entrepreneur must take care to maintain a healthy balance between work and personal life. It is a good idea to have a Plan B in case of a job cut. Motivation comes from personal satisfaction. Turbulence at work will not end, since it is part of the new work reality. Change is the only constant these days in the workplace.

The second step is to take control of your career development and to initiate a discussion on the terms of the psychological contract with your manager. This starts with an evaluation of your own market value within the context of your current employment. For this exercise, the "SWOT" (*Strengths, Weaknesses, Opportunities, Threats*) approach provides an opportunity to analyze your own strengths and weaknesses along with the opportunities and threats in your current business environment.[53] This approach serves to clarify and evaluate the potential you offer to an employer and the skills you need to perfect, in order to improve both your satisfaction at work and your career path. A SWOT analysis also forces

---

53. Mitchell Lee Marks, Philip Mirvis, and Ron Ashkenas, "Surviving M&A," *Harvard Business Review*, Vol. 95, no. 2 (March–April 2017), 145–149.

you to evaluate external forces that can impact your market value. Below are some examples of questions to ask yourself to start your analysis.

To evaluate your strengths and weaknesses:

In order to identify strengths and weaknesses, look inside yourself. How is success evaluated for the position I hold, and how do I measure it? What are my strengths? Can my colleagues or my immediate superior help me identify my strengths and my opportunities for improvement? What can I offer the company that is unique in terms of my technical expertise, my knowledge, or my interpersonal skills? What skills do I need to improve following my most recent performance appraisal? How well do I deal with change and uncertainty? How well do I tolerate the possibility of losing my job? How skilled am I at developing relationships and collaborating with my work colleagues?

Opportunities and threats are external forces that can have an impact on your development in the company.

To evaluate opportunities:

Within my company, which departments or projects are growing? Can I develop expertise that will enable me to contribute to new, interesting projects? What other positions within the organization could I apply for on a short- or medium-term basis? Are there work groups or special projects that I could take part in, so as to highlight my talents and develop new skills? What is the extent of my professional network? Do I know someone who could become my mentor? What is my market value when it comes to finding another job?

To evaluate threats:

What is the risk that I will actually lose my job? Is there a chance that my department will merge with another in which roles and responsibilities will be duplicated? Do I have the support of my supervisor? How committed am I to my position? Is a reorganization looming on the horizon?

Once you have completed your personal analysis of these four parameters, the next step is to create your personal development plan in order to define your market value, identify any new skills to develop, and find satisfaction in all aspects of your work. Then, you must plan a meeting with your supervisor to discuss mutual expectations and develop an action plan as needed. Yes, this is quite a challenge, but remember that *you* are responsible for your market value in a work environment that is competitive and constantly changing. This approach will have a positive impact on your self-confidence, your relationship with your superiors, and your perception of your position.

Overcoming a toxic work atmosphere

What leads to a toxic work environment? Contributing factors are the poor leadership of the management team and the subsequent loss of the trust the employees have in the company. People become wary of one another and constructive collegial conversation is replaced by destructive whispering about colleagues, against their bosses and against the organization. Cooperation is almost nonexistent, except for essential issues. Employees sit in isolation in front of their computers. To avoid making mistakes or being held accountable for bad decisions, they follow procedures to the letter, all in the effort to protect their jobs. Creativity and initiative get stored in the bottom drawer. Communication between the employees and their boss becomes limited or lacking. In short, the work atmosphere has become toxic.

In this context, the employee/entrepreneur has several options:

- ✓ Wait for the toxic clouds to dissipate while keeping your head low and surviving. This is a short-term solution, and not viable over the long term.
- ✓ Consider a transfer to another department. Before slamming the door, take a look around you. There may be departments in your company with a healthy work atmosphere that could provide an interesting professional challenge.
- ✓ Use your network within the company to take part in a work group or a stimulating pilot project.
- ✓ Ignore the environment and concentrate on your work. Some people are able to remain happy in this kind of environment by keeping a low profile. They tend to isolate themselves, but continue to perform because they experience deep personal satisfaction in doing their work.
- ✓ Start the process to find a new job.
- ✓ Re-evaluate your options every three months and move to Plan B if the atmosphere at work does not change.

Regardless which option you choose, it is important for you to question your implicit expectations and perceptions that are part of the psychological contract with your employer, especially when the atmosphere has become toxic. An honest and transparent discussion with your superior can clarify gray areas and answer questions. As a general rule, managers look for committed and creative employees who demonstrate leadership. As an employee, if you do not feel able to satisfy management's expectations, or if there is just no light at the end of the tunnel, you must examine the possible options. Your career and your happiness at work are in *your* hands.

Ideas for surviving post-reorganization: the survivor's toolboxes

If you decide to remain with the company, the following survivor's toolboxes may be of use to you. The proposed tools are based on testimonials collected from employees who survived one or more reorganizations. There is nothing patronizing about these suggestions, since we all have our own strengths and challenges. Solutions that succeed for one person may not be suitable for another. If you apply just one of these suggestions from either toolbox, this book will have been of use to you.

Survivor's toolbox — personal life:

15 ideas for surviving!

1. I place my personal happiness above the position I hold.

2. I strive for quality sleep, a balanced diet, and regular physical activity that have a positive impact on my stress level and capacity for resilience. (It has also been demonstrated that taking deep breaths, going for a walk, listening to calm music, exercising, and laughing, reduce the level of stress hormones.)

3. I take time to recharge following an episode of psychological fatigue. (A week of vacation is beneficial but sometimes not enough.)

4. I choose stimulating and pleasant leisure activities outside work.

5. I leave work behind at the end of every day and from Friday evening to Monday morning. I turn the work dial off.

6. I take care of myself.

7. I have positive self-esteem.

8. I'm optimistic; I see the positive side of situations.

9. I keep in touch with my friends and family and I talk with them regularly, even when I don't feel the need.

10. I know my limitations. I don't have to save the world and the company.

11. I focus my thoughts on the present, not the past.

12. I have a Plan B if I lose my job. I also have Plans C, D, and E.

13. I trust myself and my abilities.

14. I use my emotional intelligence skills optimally.

15. I live by the "golden rule": treat others the way I want to be treated.

Survivor's toolbox — work life:

20 ideas for surviving!

1. I consider myself an entrepreneur and I manage my own career even if I'm a salaried employee with a company. I develop and keep active with my professional network.

2. I work for my personal satisfaction.

3. I discuss our respective expectations under the psychological contract with my manager.

4. I'm responsible for my development and improving my skills. I make the most of all opportunities for growth. My toolbox has a lot of space! I look for a mentor if I need one.

5. I develop unique expertise that will make me indispensable, or will enable me to increase my value on the job market.

6. I'm open to possibilities for transfers on the organizational checkerboard. Too often, people tend to focus solely on promotion. A lateral transfer is a positive sign of a dynamic individual looking for new challenges for personal development.

7. I'm realistic when it comes to my expectations concerning my employer. If the business environment is slowing or changing significantly, I don't dwell on illusions.

8. I avoid getting stressed out about things over which I have no control. I choose my battles. I take a breath from time to time when the atmosphere is toxic.

9. I stay away from toxic colleagues with negative attitudes.

10. I'm resilient, and I adapt in a positive manner to adverse situations.

11. I deal with unacceptable situations actively, tactfully, and diplomatically.

12. I look at change from a positive perspective.

13. I take vacations. When possible, I take three consecutive weeks so I can recharge my batteries fully.

14. I maintain a global vision of the company's business environment and competitors.

15. I prepare myself psychologically in the event of a future reorganization.

16. I take the time to smile, laugh, and have fun. One laugh per hour!

17. I set realistic short-term goals for myself and celebrate each accomplishment when it is attained.

18. I'm a team player and contribute to an environment of mutual respect. I collaborate effectively.

19. I contribute to a positive and dynamic environment within my team.

20. I'm proactive and get involved in projects that benefit the team, while demonstrating my interest to my superior or other influential people within the organization.

Survivors' testimonials about how they overcame the reorganization

We learned a lot from the many testimonials collected to help us write this book. It was not easy for some people to share their experiences, their apprehensions, their fears, and the obstacles they had to overcome in order to survive a reorganization. We had the chance to talk with employees from all hierarchical levels within different companies or organizations. We asked them what the trigger was that influenced their decision to stay in their jobs or quit. We found that, while each situation is unique and depends on the human being and his work environment, there were also several similarities in the decision-making process of the survivors.

To that end, we observed that one important step for all survivors is to have some introspection into their personal health, their sources of stress, their work environment, their relationship with their boss, and their overall expectations. Here are some quotes from the testimonials collected.

1. *"Following a second reorganization within six months impacting a number of my direct reports, the work atmosphere had drastically changed. The company was experiencing tough times, but upper management wanted to move on and instead play the blame game on the previous leadership team. There was no acknowledgement or recognition of the stress we were enduring as a result of all the changes, and, to add insult to injury, I felt partly responsible for what the company was going through because I was a member of that previous leadership team. I was trying to be positive and supportive of my teams, but no one was being positive and supportive of me. The bond of trust with my boss was broken. I finally got to the point of deciding to leave the organization. Once I left, it took me eight months to recover well enough to even consider another position. I'm convinced that I made the right decision because I realized that I was suffering from survivor syndrome and I was no longer able to get job satisfaction in what had become a toxic work atmosphere."*
   – Executive Director

2. *"The trigger that helped me get back on my feet was a discussion with a former boss who told me, 'Trust yourself, trust yourself.' A few months later, I was transferred to another department where I had to re-establish my credibility with*

my new colleagues, since they often viewed me as a beginner without any experience. But I remembered what my former boss told me, and I trusted myself. I was successful in my new role, even though my expectations became quite different. I realized that no job is ever guaranteed."
– Marketing Manager

3. *"I dealt with the stress by developing a shell and trying to ignore the negative aspects of the work environment and emphasizing the positive joys of human relations with my colleagues and clients. I developed a Plan B for my career, by refining my business network and reflecting on other types of positions I could hold."* – Project Coordinator

4. *"I needed six months to feel better. I learned to become less of a perfectionist and cut corners when necessary. It was impossible to do everything, and I had to prioritize better. Moreover, I tried to apply a principle taught to me by a wise woman: not to get stressed out about things over which I had no control."* – Administrative Assistant

5. *"Looking back, I was able to get over things when I thought things over and took a look at myself in the mirror, realizing that I could not survive at that pace for long and would pay for it with my health. I was in denial, and I ignored my*

suffering, my stress. After a few months, colleagues spoke to me transparently and honestly, making me realize that I had burned out. With a great deal of humility, I listened to their comments and took control of my life. I did not know that I was suffering from survivor syndrome."
– Nurse

6. *"Being a survivor has a direct impact on your self-confidence. It's a difficult challenge regardless of whether you keep the same position or find yourself with new responsibilities. The day following a major reorganization, I was relieved that I had kept my job, but my self-esteem was still fragile. This 'fear' of losing my job provided me with an opportunity to reassess my skills, to question myself, and to find ways to perform in an adverse situation while striving to please myself. My bosses played an important role in helping me regain my confidence and personal satisfaction at work. A positive attitude, flexibility, resilience, and defining my personal objectives enabled me to deal with this challenge. I also learned that motivation at work does not come from my bosses; it comes from me. I've always set myself the goal of learning from each boss to help me in my career progression."* – Engineer

TO SUMMARIZE

This chapter has highlighted the importance of taking charge of your attitude and development to increase your market value in the labor market. The motivation for doing this work is intrinsic; it comes from the employee himself.[54] The psychological contract and the personal development plan are essential tools for improving the working relationship between the employee and his superiors.

Being aware of one's strengths and market value provides an invaluable sense of self-confidence when it comes to making an informed decision in the event of a reorganization or if the workplace environment becomes toxic.

A positive team atmosphere also plays an important role in overcoming the obstacles of a reorganization and avoiding the stress associated with it. Having fun and taking the time to laugh at work encourages fraternity and solidifies the sense of belonging to one's work team. As I like to say: "We are all in the same boat fighting against all odds, we might as well enjoy working together."

---

54. Bob McHardy, *Managing Effort, Getting Results,* Toronto (JM & RM Holdings, 2003), 79.

Conclusion

SURVIVING CHANGE BY THRIVING <u>THROUGH</u> CHANGE

The big winners of reorganizations are not necessarily those who keep their jobs. This reality is far too often ignored following a reorganization. The survivors are considered privileged, since they get to keep their jobs. Yet, it should be noted that the survivors have, first and foremost, had to manage the same stress as everyone else, namely the stress that was generated by the period of uncertainty before the job cuts.

It is difficult to perform well and be happy in a work environment that has become toxic because of the uncertainty over losing one's job and speculations about upcoming changes. Several employees find it difficult to deal with this period of intense stress and this has consequences on their health and their attitudes at work. Some employees develop a passive attitude by isolating themselves from others, while others become very anxious and may well burn out. Between the two extremes, there are the chameleons who swim through these troubled waters with a positive attitude, thanks to their emotional intelligence and their ability to manage stress.

And then, the moment arrives when the employee learns that he is keeping his job. The immediate reaction is one of relief, but that doesn't mean that all of the stress built up by the uncertainty leading up to the reorganization will magically disappear. The uncertainty over the possibility of losing his job is relieved on a short-term basis, but may return in a few months if rumors of reorganizations continue to loom on the horizon. Moreover, the return to work after the layoffs is challenging and brings with it new sources of stress and uncertainty for all employees. It is unrealistic to believe that all of the employees will return to work with a "business as usual" attitude, as if nothing had happened. Yet this is the message that is often conveyed by senior management. The employees do have to get back to work quickly, but management also needs to be aware of the fact that certain survivors will need support to adapt to the challenges of their new work environment.

What about the work environment following a reorganization? As a general rule, it is somewhat chaotic and has its own quota of uncertainties and questions without answers. First, there are the empty cubicles that serve as reminders of the people who have left. There is one question on all lips: how will the tasks and responsibilities of the colleagues who have left be distributed? In many cases, employees have to adjust to a new boss while feeling that they once again have to prove their worth and earn his trust. During this transition period, the employees will have to deal with the stress involved in adapting to new duties, working in a new environment and, above all, managing the additional workload. The managers are overwhelmed … and the employees are too!

This new work reality creates unexpected challenges that contribute to the development of survivor syndrome: anxiety, frustration, cynicism, the sensation of losing control, fear of making mistakes, insecurity, lack of motivation, etc. These symptoms and the resulting behaviors have an impact on the employees' personal lives and on their attitudes at work. They generally appear in the weeks following the reorganization. Then, the breach in the bond of trust between the employer and the employee must also be considered, since it generates additional stress.

Survivor syndrome is a taboo subject that is difficult to discuss openly, first and foremost because survivors are left to believe they should consider themselves lucky for keeping their jobs. One of the first manifestations is denial, since everyone thinks that the situation is temporary. Then, certain employees confide in colleagues they trust about their frustration. This discussion takes place behind closed doors, since all employees and managers want to demonstrate positive attitudes at work. We should not ignore the fact that many survivors feel distressed; they feel like they have been abandoned, are alone and powerless, and have lost control. Of the four types of survivors mentioned in Chapter 2, only the "active advocates" will come out of a reorganization with a constructive and positive attitude. And what about the other types of survivors, the "faithful followers," the "walking wounded," and the "carping critics"? Some have lost confidence in both themselves and their abilities. Others are afraid to express themselves and tend to become isolated. An employee who feels that he does not have the support of his boss will not take risks out of a fear of making mistakes. All employees need special attention from the management team in the weeks following the reorganization to minimize the effects of the survivor syndrome.

We have noted that most employees will develop positive resilience until the time when the executives seem to be insensitive with respect to their accomplishments. This situation will rapidly break the employees' trust in the managers. Then, the employees will progressively become less committed to their work, eventually achieving a disengaged attitude. The employees will do their jobs, but no more, and they will not take the interests of the company or public service to heart. Getting a demotivated and disengaged employee back on their feet requires a great deal of effort. For this reason, it is important to appoint team leaders with great emotional intelligence capabilities. Their mandate the day following a reorganization is to conduct an individual meeting with each employee, namely a discussion that is filled with transparency, empathy, realism, and sincerity. The employee should feel comfortable verbalizing his post-reorganization emotions, fears, and expectations. Time must also be set aside to discuss the details of the employee/employer psychological contract in order to clarify the expectations of each party.

In a post-reorganization context, it is essential for the employer to recognize the employees' efforts, to manage the additional workload, to celebrate small victories and, above all, to communicate with the employees frequently, in a transparent and authentic manner. A good team leader is able to recognize each employee's personality type and act in a proactive manner to limit the impacts of survivor syndrome.

We hope that this book has given you a better grasp of the many aspects of a reorganization involving job cuts, and that the testimonials provided have enabled you to make links with situations you have experienced in your work environment. Our purpose was to provide an objective analysis of the impacts of reorganizations, based on research into the matter. We have used both our professional and personal experiences and gathered several testimonials to illustrate the reality experienced by too many survivors. In order to thrive in this new reality, we propose tangible solutions to help all stakeholders.

We hope we have been successful in raising awareness among business leaders of the existence and importance of survivor syndrome and its implications for achieving the goals of a reorganization. Several actions should be considered in order to help the employees in a post-reorganization environment.

These include:
- ✓ recognizing the existence of survivor syndrome and taking action to limit its impacts
- ✓ raising the awareness of employees and managers about the behaviors and symptoms of survivor syndrome
- ✓ organizing workshops for team leaders to prepare them adequately to deal with post-reorganization challenges
- ✓ facilitating access to confidential psychological assistance to help employees who need it

Finally, we have met survivors for whom a reorganization was a stimulating and enriching challenge. These survivors manage their stress skillfully by adapting easily to changes and unexpected situations. They are resilient and can overcome difficult situations by using their emotional intelligence skills. They set personal quality of life barriers in order to escape the traps of work overload. Finding meaning in their work that brings them personal satisfaction is paramount. Mutual respect is an essential part of their relationships with colleagues. They enjoy working in a friendly team where each member is valued. Their attitude is to consider each obstacle a learning opportunity. The success of these survivors is the result of the practical application of a wide range of strategies introduced throughout the book.

In the same vein, we met several managers who did an extraordinary job of limiting the impact of a reorganization on their employees. They met with their employees frequently to establish a new psychological contract with each of them. The successful managers were able to draw on their emotional intelligence to recognize the symptoms of survivor syndrome and provide the necessary support. We have used their suggestions extensively to enrich the practical aspect of this book.

The end goal is to enable each survivor to be fulfilled and to find renewed personal satisfaction at work through ongoing enhanced performance, enriched relationships, and superior accomplishments.

Don't just survive, thrive through the change. You'll be surprised!

SUGGESTED READINGS

Aon Corporation. "2018 Trends in Global Employee Engagement." published by Aon, www.aon.com. Last visited: August 7, 2019.

Aon Corporation. "Managing Employee Engagement During Times of Change." June 2013, www.aon.com. Last visited: August 7, 2019.

Becdach, C. et al. "Rethinking the Rules of Reorganization." McKinsey & Company, April 2016. www.mckinsey.com. Last visited: August 7, 2019.

Bisson-Desrochers, A. "Protective Factors and Our Resilience Toolbox." *Mammoth Magazine*, No. 13, Summer 2013, 10. www.humanstress.ca. Last visited: August 7, 2019.

Bourdon, O. "Resilience: When Hope Becomes Possible for Everyone." *Mammoth Magazine*, No. 13, Summer 2013, 2. www.humanstress.ca. Last visited: August 7, 2019.

Bradberry, T. et al. "Emotional Intelligence 2.0." TalentSmart, San Diego, 2009.

Bradberry, T. "11 Signs That You Lack Emotional Intelligence." TalentSmart Newsletter Article. www.talentsmart.com. Last visited: August 7, 2019.

Bradberry, T. "8 Ways Cutthroat Work Cultures Suck the Life Out of You." www.huffingtonpost.ca. January 27, 2018. Last visited: August 7, 2019.

Buckingham, Marcus and Ashley Goodall. "The Power of Hidden Teams." *Harvard Business Review*, https://hbr.org/cover-story/2019/05/the-power-of-hidden-teams. May 2019.

Cross, R. et al. "Collaborative Overload." *Harvard Business Review*, Vol. 94, No. 1/2, January–February 2016.

Fournies F. *Coaching for Improved Work Performance*. McGraw-Hill, New York, 2000.

Girod, S. J. G. "Restructure or Reconfigure?" *Harvard Business Review*, Vol. 95, No. 2, March–April 2017.

Goleman, D. *Emotional Intelligence*. Bantam, New York, 1995.

Harter, Jim. "Dismal Employee Management is a Sign of Global Mismanagement." December 20, 2017. http://news.gallup.com. Last visited: August 7, 2019.

Heidari-Robinson, S. and S. Heywood. "Getting Reorgs Right." *Harvard Business Review*, Vol. 94, No. 11, November 2016.

Juster, R-P. et al. "Stress and Resilience." *Mammoth Magazine*, No. 13, Summer 2013, 6.

Johnson, S. et al. "Pioneers, Drivers, Integrators, and Guardians." *Harvard Business Review*, Vol. 95, No. 2, March–April 2017.

Kotter, John P. and Dan S. Cohen. *The Heart of Change*. Harvard Business Review Press, Boston, 2002.

Kupec, Amy J. "Overcoming the Survivor's Syndrome: Current Theories and Practices." College of Liberal Arts & Social Sciences, Theses and Dissertations. Paper 67. 2010. http://via.library.depaul.edu/etd/67. Last visited: August 7, 2019.

Lipkin, Mike. "How to Become a Champion Collaborator." http://www.mikelipkin.com/how-to-become-a-champion-collaborator/. Last visited: August 7, 2019.

Lupien, Sonia. *Well Stressed: Manage Stress Before it Turns Toxic.* Harper Collins e-books, Toronto, 2012.

Lupien, Sonia. "Deconstructing and Reconstructing Stress." *Mammoth Magazine*, No. 16, Autumn 2016. www.humanstress.ca. Last visited: August 7, 2019.

Marks, M. L. et al. "Surviving M&A." *Harvard Business Review*, Vol. 95, No. 2, March–April 2017.

McHardy, Bob. *Managing Effort, Getting Results.* JM & RM Holdings, Toronto, 2003.

McKee, Anne. "Happiness Traps: How we Sabotage Ourselves at Work." *Harvard Business Review*, Vol. 95, No. 5, September–October 2017.

Mishra, Aneil K. et al. "Downsizing the Company Without Downsizing Morale." *MIT Sloan Management Review*, Spring 2009. www.sloanreview.mit.edu. Last visited: August 7, 2019.

Mizne, David. "5 Surprising Signs of a Disengaged Employee." www.15five.com. Last visited: August 7, 2019.

Momm, T. "It Pays to Have an Eye for Emotions: Emotion Recognition Ability Indirectly Predicts Annual Income." *Journal of Organizational Behavior*, Nov. 2014.

Nink, Marco et al. "Can Bad Managers be Saved?" December 21, 2016. http://news.gallup.com. Last visited: August 7, 2019.

Noer, David M. *Healing the Wounds.* Jossey-Bass, San Francisco, 1993.

Sandberg, Sheryl and Adam Grant. *Option B: Facing Adversity, Building Resilience, and Finding Joy.* Alfred A. Knopf, New York, 2017.

Sorenson, Susan and Garman, Keri. "How to Tackle U.S. Employees' Stagnating Engagement." *Gallup Business Journal*, June 11 2013. http://news.gallup.com. Last visited: August 7, 2019.

Sucher, Sandra J. and Shalene Gupta. "Layoffs That Don't Break Your Company." *Harvard Business Review*, Vol. 96, No. 3, May–June 2018.

ACKNOWLEDGMENTS

There are always a number of people who contribute to the development of a manuscript, and this book is no exception. First and foremost, we are indebted to those who willingly shared their personal experiences and emotional challenges of overcoming a reorganization at work. The number of examples we could draw from confirmed for us that we were on the right path addressing this topic.

The writing of this book started out in French. Nicole wrote an early version titled *Comment survivre à une réorganisation au travail* published in French by les Éditions au Carré. Nicole then asked a professional translator, Sheryl Curtis, to translate it into English. Many thanks to Sheryl for her great contribution in getting us started on the path to this book.

While we could draw on our personal experiences to inform our thinking on the topic of survivor syndrome, we also relied on several people with expertise in human resources and change management to review the manuscript and provide their input. We are grateful to all of you.

We also want to recognize and thank the important contributions of all the reviewers of our book. Whether it was the wording of a sentence, a topic suggestion, or a correction, the feedback was welcomed and valuable. We are so fortunate to have so many willing and interested supporters of our project. A big thank you to each and every one of you.

ABOUT THE AUTHORS

Nicole Labbe, born in Montreal, has always been passionate about human relations and communications. She worked for a large pharmaceutical company for twenty-five years, where she held several sales and marketing positions, including extensive experience as a team manager in a changing environment. Through seven different reorganizations involving job cuts and organizational changes, she experienced uncertainty and—the day following each reorganization—repeatedly found herself with a new team that she had to get to know and motivate. She well understands the impact of reorganizations on employees at all levels of a business. She is now retired and has embraced her new career as a consultant and speaker on how to overcome the challenges of "surviving" a reorg at work.

Christine Strobele, from Sudbury, Ontario, has enjoyed a career spanning over thirty years in the pharmaceutical and biotechnology sectors. She has witnessed significant industry changes and has been swept up in many reorganizations. Often, she became responsible for damage control for the fractured team left behind. From these experiences, Christine has developed a keen interest in survivor syndrome, and acknowledges it can have lasting effects. For others going through similar situations, she wants to offer early intervention advice to recognize, address, and overcome these feelings. Writing this book created the opportunity to share some practical and simple solutions that helped her find renewed enjoyment at work.

Nicole Labbe and Christine Strobele are available for select speaking engagements.

To inquire about a possible appearance, please visit www.nicole-labbe.com